WEST PUBLISHING COMPANY

P.O. Box 3526

St. Paul, Minnesota 55165

August, 1981

Administrative Law and Process, 2nd Ed., 1981, approx. 440 pages, by Ernest Gellhorn, Professor of Law, University of Virginia and Barry B. Boyer, Professor of Law, SUNY, Buffalo.

Agency-Partnership, 1977, 364 pages, by Roscoe T. Steffen, Late Professor of Law, University of Chicago.

American Indian Law, 1981, 288 pages, by William C. Canby, Jr., former Professor of Law, Arizona State University.

Antitrust Law and Economics, 2nd Ed., 1981, 425 pages, by Ernest Gellhorn, Professor of Law, University of Virginia.

Church-State Relations—Law of 1981, 305 pages, by Leonard F. Manning, Professor of Law, Fordham University.

Civil Procedure, 1979, 271 pages, by Mary Kay Kane, Professor of Law, University of California, Hastings College of the Law.

Civil Rights, 1978, 279 pages, by Norman Vieira, Professor of Law, University of Idaho.

Commercial Paper, 2nd Ed., 1975, 361 pages, by Charles M. Weber, Professor of Business Law, University of Arizona.

Conflicts, 3rd Ed., 1974, 432 pages, by Albert A. Ehrenzweig, Late Professor of Law, University of California, Berkeley.

NUTSHELL SERIES

Constitutional Analysis, 1979, 388 pages, by Jerre S. Williams, former Professor of Law, University of Texas.

Constitutional Power—Federal and State, 1974, 411 pages, by David E. Engdahl, former Professor of Law, University of Denver.

Consumer Law, 2nd Ed., 1981, 418 pages, by David G. Epstein, Dean and Professor of Law, University of Arkansas and Steve H. Nickles, Professor of Law, University of Arkansas.

Contracts, 1975, 307 pages, by Gordon D. Schaber, Dean and Professor of Law, McGeorge School of Law and Claude D. Rohwer, Professor of Law, McGeorge School of Law.

Contract Remedies, 1981, approx. 325 pages, by Jane M. Friedman, Professor of Law, Wayne State University.

Corporations—Law of, 1980, 379 pages, by Robert W. Hamilton, Professor of Law, University of Texas.

Corrections and Prisoners' Rights—Law of, 1976, 353 pages, by Sheldon Krantz, Professor of Law, Boston University.

Criminal Law, 1975, 302 pages, by Arnold H. Loewy, Professor of Law, University of North Carolina.

Criminal Procedure—Constitutional Limitations, 3rd Ed., 1980, 438 pages, by Jerold H. Israel, Professor of Law, University of Michigan and Wayne R. LaFave, Professor of Law, University of Illinois.

Debtor-Creditor Law, 2nd Ed., 1980, 324 pages, by David G. Epstein, Dean and Professor of Law, University of Arkansas.

Employment Discrimination—Federal Law of, 2nd Ed., 1981, 402 pages, by Mack A. Player, Professor of Law, University of Georgia.

NUTSHELL SERIES

Energy Law, 1981, approx. 330 pages, by Joseph P. Tomain, Professor of Law, Drake University.

Estate Planning—Introduction to, 2nd Ed., 1978, 378 pages, by Robert J. Lynn, Professor of Law, Ohio State University.

Evidence, Federal Rules of, 1981, 428 pages, by Michael H. Graham, Professor of Law, University of Illinois.

Evidence, State and Federal Rules, 2nd Ed., 1981, 514 pages, by Paul F. Rothstein, Professor of Law, Georgetown University.

Family Law, 1977, 400 pages, by Harry D. Krause, Professor of Law, University of Illinois.

Federal Estate and Gift Taxation, 2nd Ed., 1979, 488 pages, by John K. McNulty, Professor of Law, University of California, Berkeley.

Federal Income Taxation of Individuals, 2nd Ed., 1978, 422 pages, by John K. McNulty, Professor of Law, University of California, Berkeley.

Federal Income Taxation of Corporations and Stockholders, 2nd Ed., 1981, 362 pages, by Jonathan Sobeloff, Late Professor of Law, Georgetown University and Peter P. Weidenbruch, Jr., Professor of Law, Georgetown University.

Federal Jurisdiction, 2nd Ed., 1981, 258 pages, by David P. Currie, Professor of Law, University of Chicago.

Future Interests, 1981, 361 pages, by Lawrence W. Waggoner, Professor of Law, University of Michigan.

Government Contracts, 1979, 423 pages, by W. Noel Keyes, Professor of Law, Pepperdine University.

Historical Introduction to Anglo-American Law, 2nd Ed., 1973, 280 pages, by Frederick G. Kempin, Jr., Professor of Business Law, Wharton School of Finance and Commerce, University of Pennsylvania.

Injunctions, 1974, 264 pages, by John F. Dobbyn, Professor of Law, Villanova University.

Insurance Law, 1981, 281 pages, by John F. Dobbyn, Professor of Law, Villanova University.

International Business Transactions, 1981, 393 pages, by Donald T. Wilson, Professor of Law, Loyola University, Los Angeles.

Judicial Process, 1980, 292 pages, by William L. Reynolds, Professor of Law, University of Maryland.

Jurisdiction, 4th Ed., 1980, 232 pages, by Albert A. Ehrenzweig, Late Professor of Law, University of California, Berkeley, David W. Louisell, Late Professor of Law, University of California, Berkeley and Geoffrey C. Hazard, Jr., Professor of Law, Yale Law School.

Juvenile Courts, 2nd Ed., 1977, 275 pages, by Sanford J. Fox, Professor of Law, Boston College.

Labor Arbitration Law and Practice, 1979, 358 pages, by Dennis R. Nolan, Professor of Law, University of South Carolina.

Labor Law, 1979, 403 pages, by Douglas L. Leslie, Professor of Law, University of Virginia.

Land Use, 1978, 316 pages, by Robert R. Wright, Professor of Law, University of Arkansas, Little Rock and Susan Webber, Professor of Law, University of Arkansas, Little Rock.

Landlord and Tenant Law, 1979, 319 pages, by David S. Hill, Professor of Law, University of Colorado.

Law Study and Law Examinations—Introduction to, 1971, 389 pages, by Stanley V. Kinyon, Late Professor of Law, University of Minnesota.

Legal Interviewing and Counseling, 1976, 353 pages, by Thomas L. Shaffer, Professor of Law, Washington and Lee University.

NUTSHELL SERIES

Legal Research, 3rd Ed., 1978, 415 pages, by Morris L. Cohen, Professor of Law and Law Librarian, Yale University.

Legislative Law and Process, 1975, 279 pages, by Jack Davies, Professor of Law, William Mitchell College of Law.

Local Government Law, 1975, 386 pages, by David J. McCarthy, Jr., Dean and Professor of Law, Georgetown University.

Mass Communications Law, 1977, 431 pages, by Harvey L. Zuckman, Professor of Law, Catholic University and Martin J. Gaynes, Lecturer in Law, Temple University.

Medical Malpractice—The Law of, 1977, 340 pages, by Joseph H. King, Professor of Law, University of Tennessee.

Military Law, 1980, 378 pages, by Charles A. Shanor, Professor of Law, Emory University and Timothy P. Terrell, Professor of Law, Emory University.

Post-Conviction Remedies, 1978, 360 pages, by Robert Popper, Professor of Law, University of Missouri, Kansas City.

Presidential Power, 1977, 328 pages, by Arthur Selwyn Miller, Professor of Law Emeritus, George Washington University.

Procedure Before Trial, 1972, 258 pages, by Delmar Karlen, Professor of Law, College of William and Mary.

Products Liability, 2nd Ed., 1981, 341 pages, by Dix W. Noel, Late Professor of Law, University of Tennessee and Jerry J. Phillips, Professor of Law, University of Tennessee.

NUTSHELL SERIES

Professional Responsibility, 1980, 399 pages, by Robert H. Aronson, Professor of Law, University of Washington, and Donald T. Weckstein, Professor of Law, University of San Diego.

Real Estate Finance, 1979, 292 pages, by Jon W. Bruce, Professor of Law, Stetson University.

Real Property, 2nd Ed., 1981, approx. 440 pages, by Roger H. Bernhardt, Professor of Law, Golden Gate University.

Remedies, 1977, 364 pages, by John F. O'Connell, Professor of Law, Western State University College of Law, Fullerton.

Res Judicata, 1976, 310 pages, by Robert C. Casad, Professor of Law, University of Kansas.

Sales, 2nd Ed., 1981, 370 pages, by John M. Stockton, Professor of Business Law, Wharton School of Finance and Commerce, University of Pennsylvania.

Secured Transactions, 2nd Ed., 1981, 391 pages, by Henry J. Bailey, Professor of Law, Willamette University.

Securities Regulation, 1978, 300 pages, by David L. Ratner, Professor of Law, Cornell University.

Titles—The Calculus of Interests, 1968, 277 pages, by Oval A. Phipps, Late Professor of Law, St. Louis University.

Torts—Injuries to Persons and Property, 1977, 434 pages by Edward J. Kionka, Professor of Law, Southern Illinois University.

Torts—Injuries to Family, Social and Trade Relations, 1979, 358 pages, by Wex S. Malone, Professor of Law Emeritus, Louisiana State University.

Hornbook Series
and
Basic Legal Texts
of

WEST PUBLISHING COMPANY

P.O. Box 3526

St. Paul, Minnesota 55165

August, 1981

HORNBOOKS & BASIC TEXTS

Common Law Pleading, Koffler and Reppy's Hornbook on, 1969, 663 pages, by Joseph H. Koffler, Professor of Law, New York Law School and Alison Reppy, Late Dean and Professor of Law, New York Law School.

Common Law Pleading, Shipman's Hornbook on, 3rd Ed., 1923, 644 pages, by Henry W. Ballantine, Late Professor of Law, University of California, Berkeley.

Constitutional Law, Nowak, Rotunda and Young's Hornbook on, 1978 with 1979 Pocket Part, 974 pages, by John E. Nowak, Professor of Law, University of Illinois, Ronald D. Rotunda, Professor of Law, University of Illinois, and J. Nelson Young, Professor of Law, University of Illinois.

Contracts, Calamari and Perillo's Hornbook on, 2nd Ed., 1977, 878 pages, by John D. Calamari, Professor of Law, Fordham University and Joseph M. Perillo, Professor of Law, Fordham University.

Contracts, Corbin's One Volume Student Ed., 1952, 1224 pages, by Arthur L. Corbin, Late Professor of Law, Yale University.

Contracts, Simpson's Hornbook on, 2nd Ed., 1965, 510 pages, by Laurence P. Simpson, Late Professor of Law, New York University.

Corporate Taxation, Kahn's Handbook on, 3rd Ed., Student Ed., Soft cover, 1981, 614 pages, by Douglas A. Kahn, Professor of Law, University of Michigan.

Corporations, Henn's Hornbook on, 2nd Ed., 1970, 956 pages, by Harry G. Henn, Professor of Law, Cornell University.

Criminal Law, LaFave and Scott's Hornbook on, 1972, 763 pages, by Wayne R. LaFave, Professor of Law, University of Illinois, and Austin Scott, Jr., Late Professor of Law, University of Colorado.

Damages, McCormick's Hornbook on, 1935, 811 pages, by Charles T. McCormick, Late Dean and Professor of Law, University of Texas.

Domestic Relations, Clark's Hornbook on, 1968, 754 pages, by Homer H. Clark, Jr., Professor of Law, University of Colorado.

Environmental Law, Rodgers' Hornbook on, 1977, 956 pages, by William H. Rodgers, Jr., Professor of Law, University of Washington.

Equity, McClintock's Hornbook on, 2nd Ed., 1948, 643 pages, by Henry L. McClintock, Late Professor of Law, University of Minnesota.

Estate and Gift Taxes, Lowndes, Kramer and McCord's Hornbook on, 3rd Ed., 1974, 1099 pages, by Charles L. B. Lowndes, Late Professor of Law, Duke University, Robert Kramer, Professor of Law Emeritus, George Washington University, and John H. McCord, Professor of Law, University of Illinois.

Evidence, Lilly's Introduction to, 1978, 486 pages, by Graham C. Lilly, Professor of Law, University of Virginia.

Evidence, McCormick's Hornbook on, 2nd Ed., 1972 with 1978 Pocket Part, 938 pages, General Editor, Edward W. Cleary, Professor of Law Emeritus, Arizona State University.

Federal Courts, Wright's Hornbook on, 3rd Ed., 1976, 818 pages, including Federal Rules Appendix, by Charles Alan Wright, Professor of Law, University of Texas.

Future Interest, Simes' Hornbook on, 2nd Ed., 1966, 355 pages, by Lewis M. Simes, Late Professor of Law, University of Michigan.

Income Taxation, Chommie's Hornbook on, 2nd Ed., 1973, 1051 pages, by John C. Chommie, Late Professor of Law, University of Miami.

Insurance, Keeton's Basic Text on, 1971, 712 pages, by Robert E. Keeton, former Professor of Law, Harvard University.

Labor Law, Gorman's Basic Text on, 1976, 914 pages, by Robert A. Gorman, Professor of Law, University of Pennsylvania.

Law Problems, Ballentine's, 5th Ed., 1975, 767 pages, General Editor, William E. Burby, Professor of Law Emeritus, University of Southern California.

Legal Writing Style, Weihofen's, 2nd Ed., 1980, 332 pages, by Henry Weihofen, Professor of Law Emeritus, University of New Mexico.

New York Practice, Siegel's Hornbook on, 1978, with 1979-80 Pocket Part, 1011 pages, by David D. Siegel, Professor of Law, Albany Law School of Union University.

Oil and Gas, Hemingway's Hornbook on, 1971 with 1979 Pocket Part, 486 pages, by Richard W. Hemingway, Professor of Law, University of Oklahoma.

Partnership, Crane and Bromberg's Hornbook on, 1968, 695 pages, by Alan R. Bromberg, Professor of Law, Southern Methodist University.

Poor, Law of the, LaFrance, Schroeder, Bennett and Boyd's Hornbook on, 1973, 558 pages, by Arthur B. LaFrance, Professor of Law, University of Maine, Milton R. Schroeder, Professor of Law, Arizona State University, Robert W. Bennett, Professor of Law, Northwestern University and William E. Boyd, Professor of Law, University of Arizona.

HORNBOOKS & BASIC TEXTS

Property, Boyer's Survey of, 3rd Ed., 1981, 766 pages, by Ralph E. Boyer, Professor of Law, University of Miami.

Real Estate Finance Law, Osborne, Nelson and Whitman's Hornbook on, (successor to Hornbook on Mortgages), 1979, 885 pages, by George E. Osborne, Late Professor of Law, Stanford University, Grant S. Nelson, Professor of Law, University of Missouri, Columbia and Dale A. Whitman, Professor of Law, University of Washington.

Real Property, Burby's Hornbook on, 3rd Ed., 1965, 490 pages, by William E. Burby, Professor of Law Emeritus, University of Southern California.

Real Property, Moynihan's Introduction to, 1962, 254 pages, by Cornelius J. Moynihan, Professor of Law, Suffolk University.

Remedies, Dobbs' Hornbook on, 1973, 1067 pages, by Dan B. Dobbs, Professor of Law, University of Arizona.

Sales, Nordstrom's Hornbook on, 1970, 600 pages, by Robert J. Nordstrom, former Professor of Law, Ohio State University.

Secured Transactions under the U.C.C., Henson's Hornbook on, 2nd Ed., 1979, with 1979 Pocket Part, 504 pages, by Ray D. Henson, Professor of Law, University of California, Hastings College of the Law.

Torts, Prosser's Hornbook on, 4th Ed., 1971, 1208 pages, by William L. Prosser, Late Dean and Professor of Law, University of California, Berkeley.

Trial Advocacy, Jeans' Handbook on, Student Ed., Soft cover, 1975, by James W. Jeans, Professor of Law, University of Missouri, Kansas City.

HORNBOOKS & BASIC TEXTS

Trusts, Bogert's Hornbook on, 5th Ed., 1973, 726 pages, by George G. Bogert, Late Professor of Law, University of Chicago and George T. Bogert, Attorney, Chicago, Illinois.

Urban Planning and Land Development Control, Hagman's Hornbook on, 1971, 706 pages, by Donald G. Hagman, Professor of Law, University of California, Los Angeles.

Uniform Commercial Code, White and Summers' Hornbook on, 2nd Ed., 1980, 1250 pages, by James J. White, Professor of Law, University of Michigan and Robert S. Summers, Professor of Law, Cornell University.

Wills, Atkinson's Hornbook on, 2nd Ed., 1953, 975 pages, by Thomas E. Atkinson, Late Professor of Law, New York University.

Advisory Board

Professor JESSE H. CHOPER
University of California School of Law, Berkeley

Professor DAVID P. CURRIE
University of Chicago Law School

Dean DAVID G. EPSTEIN
University of Arkansas School of Law

Professor ERNEST GELLHORN
University of Virginia School of Law

Professor YALE KAMISAR
University of Michigan Law School

Professor WAYNE R. LaFAVE
University of Illinois College of Law

Professor RICHARD C. MAXWELL
Duke University School of Law

Professor ARTHUR R. MILLER
Harvard University Law School

Professor JAMES J. WHITE
University of Michigan Law School

Professor CHARLES ALAN WRIGHT
University of Texas School of Law

LABOR
ARBITRATION LAW
AND
PRACTICE

IN A NUTSHELL

By
DENNIS R. NOLAN
Associate Professor of Law
University of South Carolina

ST. PAUL, MINN.
WEST PUBLISHING CO.
1979

Library of Congress Cataloging in Publication Data

Nolan, Dennis R   · 1945–
    Labor arbitration law and practice in a nutshell.
    (Nutshell series)
    Includes index.
    1. Arbitration, Industrial—United States.
I. Title.
KF3425.N64   344'.73'018914   79–4316

ISBN 0–8299–2032–3

Nolan Labor Arbitration Law
1st Reprint—1982

For Joseph L. Nolan,

Without whom this book
could not have been written

*

XVII

PREFACE

This book is not intended as a substitute for classroom instruction in labor arbitration, still less for practical experience in the field. Nor is it intended to (or could it) take the place of the detailed treatises on labor arbitration already available to the practitioner and scholar. Its purpose is much narrower, to provide a simple but comprehensive description of the origin, development and practice of labor arbitration in America. Ideally this overview will serve as an introduction to more thorough study in other forms.

Even this limited purpose requires a good bit of detail. The major issues in labor arbitration law are presented at length to permit a full exploration of their importance and of the conflicting opinions on them. Every effort has been made to be fair, but inevitably some personal beliefs have made their way into the text. Most of these are clearly identifiable as such, and can be evaluated accordingly.

Many people contributed to this book in different ways: students in my classes, who helped me clarify issues; research assistants, who found even the most obscure cases and texts; colleagues who provided advice gladly and frankly; deans who made available needed support for this project; secretaries who typed draft after draft without complaint; and a family that did not begrudge the hours lost to "the book." Among all of these, one is deserving of special mention: Professor Roger Abrams of Case Western Reserve University, an able scholar and arbitrator, offered extensive comments on an earlier draft of this work and saved me from innumerable errors both large and small. I am deeply indebted to him and to the others who were of such help.

Finally, I am grateful to the American Arbitration Association, the Federal Mediation and Conciliation Service, and the National Academy of Arbitrators for permission to quote from or reprint these items:

> American Arbitration Association, *Labor Arbitration Procedures and Techniques* (no date), *Voluntary Labor Arbitration Rules* (no date) and the current AAA forms in Appendix 1.

> American Arbitration Association, Federal Mediation and Conciliation Service, and National Academy of Arbitrators, *Code of Professional Responsibility for Arbitrators of Labor-Management Disputes* (1974).

DENNIS R. NOLAN

Columbia, South Carolina
April, 1979

OUTLINE

XXVIII

*

TABLE OF CASES

References are to Pages

TABLE OF CASES

TABLE OF CASES

TABLE OF CASES

TABLE OF STATUTES

References are to Pages

*

LABOR ARBITRATION LAW
AND
PRACTICE
IN A NUTSHELL

I

THE DEVELOPMENT OF THE LABOR ARBITRATION PROCESS

A. A DEFINITION OF THE CONCEPT

Arbitration is a procedure in which parties to a dispute voluntarily agree to be bound by the decision of an impartial person outside of the normal judicial process. That impartial person, the arbitrator, is expected to make his decision on the basis of evidence and arguments presented by the parties. Arbitration thus resembles a judicial proceeding in form, but is usually conducted with less formality and ordinarily does not involve government officials.

Labor arbitration is simply the arbitration of a dispute between an employer and the union representing his employees involving some aspect of the employment relationship. Such disputes are of two types: (1) "interest" disputes, involving disagreements over the terms to be included in a contract (called a "collective bargaining agreement") between the employer and the union representing his employees; and (2) "rights" or "grievance" disputes, involving disagreements over the meaning or application of terms already contained in a collective bargaining agreement. Unless otherwise stated, the discussion in this book concerns grievance arbitration. Interest arbitration will be treated in a separate section below.

B. THE ORIGINS OF LABOR ARBITRATION

The logic and simplicity of arbitration have commended that process to men from the earliest times. Mythology tells us, for example, that Venus, Juno and Pallas Athene agreed to allow Paris to decide their dispute over which of them was the most beautiful. Primitive societies have long favored resolution of disputes by impartial arbitration, frequently to the exclusion of any formal legal process. The arbitration process appears in the Norse sagas, among American Indian tribes and in the early Christian community (see I Cor.

VI, 5). For the same reasons arbitration was widely accepted as an adjunct to the formal law of the Romans and was the preferred means of settlement of commercial disputes of the Middle Ages.

With this background it should be no surprise that as industrialization led to an increase in the frequency of labor disputes, arbitration was suggested as a remedy. As early as 1786 the Chamber of Commerce of New York organized an arbitration tribunal to resolve a dispute over seamen's wages. There were a few other labor arbitrations in those early years, but it was not a common phenomenon until the second half of the Nineteenth Century. Private tribunals for the settlement of labor disputes were organized in England in the 1860's and in the 1870's arbitrations were held in the Pittsburgh iron trade, the Massachusetts shoe industry and the Appalachian coal fields.

The arbitration process was familiar enough by the 1880's to be recognized in the laws of a number of states. Typically these laws simply authorized the courts to appoint local boards of arbitration upon the joint request of employers and employees. By 1901, sixteen states had enacted such laws. The federal government also passed laws dealing with arbitration, chiefly for the railroad industry and for war-time labor disputes. These state and federal laws are discussed in more detail below.

It should be emphasized that for a long time the term "arbitration" had meanings far removed from the quasi-judicial process we know today. Originally demands for arbitration were really requests for employer recognition of and negotiation with unions. Later "arbitration" came to mean something akin to what is now known as "mediation"—that is, the use of an impartial person to help the parties communicate and reach their own agreement. Still later after several industries had appointed permanent "impartial chairmen," the term began to take on its modern meaning, but even then the impartial chairmen most frequently engaged in "consensus arbitration," a mixture of mediation and quasi-judicial arbitration. Indeed, it is only in the last generation or so, with the decline in the percentage of "impartial chairmen" and a vast increase in the use of *ad hoc* arbitrators, that parties have come to treat the arbitrator as a judge rather than a peacemaker.

Recently, there has been a virtual explosion in the use of labor arbitration. Well over 90% of all collective bargaining agreements contain provisions for some form of arbitration, and these provisions are being used more often than ever before.

II

ARBITRATION PROCEDURE

A. CONTRACTUAL REQUIREMENTS

1. In General

The most important fact to keep in mind about arbitration is that it is a *contractual* process. With the exception of mandatory arbitration laws covering a few public employees, labor arbitration occurs only because parties to a dispute have agreed to it, either in a current collective bargaining agreement or as an *ad hoc* measure. Because it is the creation of the parties, it can take any form those parties wish to give it; there is, in other words, no single model the parties must adopt. On the other hand there are a relatively small number of models which the vast bulk of disputing parties do in fact adopt, either because of the effectiveness of those models or because of their familiarity. The parties can either spell out the agreed-upon arbitration procedure in their own words or can incorporate an established procedure by reference. This section will discuss some of the problems involved in drafting an appropriate submission agreement or arbitration clause.

2. The Submission Agreement

Where parties to a dispute do not have in effect a contract clause mandating a certain arbitration procedure, they may nevertheless agree to submit a particular dispute to arbitration. This is not a frequent occurrence, but it does happen from time to time. In such cases arbitration is initiated by signing a "submission agreement," which is simply a document stating the nature of the dispute and affirming the parties' intention to arbitrate and to abide by the arbitrator's award. The submission agreement constitutes a contract to arbitrate; it therefore establishes the extent of the arbitrator's authority. At the same time it informs the arbitrator of the issues in dispute, the positions of the parties on those issues, and the relief sought. The submission agreement, if carefully drafted, should also describe the procedure to be followed by the arbitrator— for example, whether there is to be a single arbitrator or a panel, when, where, and how hearings are to take place, and so on. Because these points should be addressed in an arbitration clause, they are discussed below in that context. Ideally the submission agreement should be as detailed as an arbitration clause. Because of the *ad hoc* nature of disputes in which submission agreements are used, they usually are not so carefully drawn.

3. *The Arbitration Clause*

The arbitration clause is a provision in a collective bargaining agreement requiring that disputes arising out of or relating to the agreement be settled by arbitration. It should also define the arbitration process agreed to in such a manner that it can be easily utilized when disputes arise, without confusion over the process itself. To achieve this objective the arbitration clause should answer at least the following questions.* In practice, arbitration clauses are seldom this detailed.

WHAT_____

_____is to be arbitrated?

_____are the duties and obligations of each party?

HOW_____

_____is arbitration initiated?

_____are arbitrators appointed and vacancies filled?

_____are time and place for hearings fixed?

_____are hearings opened? Closed? Reopened?

_____are costs controlled?

WHEN_____

_____are arbitrators appointed?

_____must hearings begin?

_____must the award be rendered?

* The following list is from American Arbitration Association, *Labor Arbitration Procedures and Techniques* 7 (No date).

WHERE_____

_____are notice, documents and correspondence to be sent?

_____shall hearings be held?

_____is the award to be delivered?

WHO_____

_____administers the arbitration?

_____keeps the records and makes technical preparations?

_____gives notice of hearings and other matters?

_____appoints the arbitrators if the parties cannot agree?

_____fills vacancies on arbitration boards when necessary?

_____grants adjournments?

Very likely the parties will want to address other questions as well, particularly those involving the procedure to be followed before a problem goes to arbitration (commonly called the grievance procedure).

It is quite possible to draft a clause answering such questions and there are many books which provide models and advice. The following pages deal with some of the major issues to be considered while drafting and negotiating an arbitration clause. If the parties are primarily interested in making arbitration a reality and are relatively unconcerned with the details of the procedure, they would be well advised to incorporate *in toto* or by reference some set of rules that has been tested by the experience of others. Another collective bargaining agreement might provide a suitable reference point, but because another contract is likely to reflect the peculiarities of the relationship between the parties to it, a more objective model should be sought. The American Arbitration Association (AAA), a private, non-profit organization dedicated to the improvement and expansion of the arbitration process, has developed a set of *Voluntary Labor Arbitration Rules* (reprinted in Appendix 2) that serves as a good starting place. The parties may well want to modify some of these rules to reflect their own beliefs, desires or circumstances, but they could simply adopt the AAA Rules by reference in a clause such as the following, which is recommended by the AAA:

> Any dispute, claim or grievance arising out of or relating to the interpretation or the application of this agreement shall be submitted to arbitration under the Voluntary Labor Arbitration Rules of the American Arbitration Association. The parties further agree to accept the arbitrator's award as final and binding upon them.*

* American Arbitration Association, *Labor Arbitration Procedures and Techniques* 7 (No date).

Because the AAA rules are relatively precise and objective, frequent reference will be made to them throughout this book.

B. INITIATION OF ARBITRATION

1. The Demand for Arbitration

Arbitration may be initiated either by a submission signed by both parties, as discussed above, or by the demand of one party to an arbitration clause. This "demand for arbitration" is simply a formal request, usually in writing, made by one party to the other for arbitration of a particular dispute pursuant to the arbitration clause of the collective bargaining agreement between them. A copy of the demand should be sent to the group designated in the arbitration clause as the appropriate administrative body. Usually this will mean the AAA or the Federal Mediation and Conciliation Service (FMCS), an agency of the federal government, but might mean a state or local government agency. (See Appendix 1, Form 1, for the AAA demand form).

The demand must comply with any procedural requirements established in the arbitration clause. Time limits must be followed, for example, and the party seeking arbitration should be careful to avoid raising in the demand issues which have not yet been considered in the earlier steps of the grievance procedure. Failure to abide by these requirements might result in loss of arbitration rights on that issue (in the technical term, the issue might not be "arbitrable"). As stated, arbitration depends for its force on the previous agreement of the parties and if that agreement sets up procedural requirements those requirements must be met before arbitration is required or appropriate.

To be complete, the demand should include the following items:

(a) Names and addresses of both parties (if the demand is also submitted to an administrative organization; the parties presumably already have this information).

(b) The effective dates of the collective bargaining agreement and the text of the arbitration clause.

(c) A brief statement of the issue or issues to be arbitrated and the relief sought, including, where appropriate, names, dates and numbers. (Note: the demand simply phrases the issue. It is not an appropriate place for argument or evidence. Save such matters for the hearing.)

(d) The dated signature of the union or company official authorized to demand arbitration.

2. *The Reply*

The responding party may submit a reply to the demand, briefly setting forth its position on the claim of the demanding party. Where an administrative organization such as the AAA is involved, a reply will ordinarily be sought as a matter of course. Unless the arbitration clause provides otherwise, a reply is not required and in its absence the claim will be deemed to be denied.

The demand and the reply will be read by the arbitrator at the beginning of the arbitration hearing. Because the arbitrator will normally have no other knowledge of the dispute before evidence is presented, these two documents will guide him in his decisions during the hearing. Because his authority is limited to the questions presented to him, the demand and reply may also provide the boundaries of his award, although this is more often done by an agreed-upon statement of the issue at the beginning of the arbitration. The demand and reply should therefore frame the issues on which the arbitrator's decision is sought with as much precision as possible. If there is no formal demand and reply, their functions may be served by providing the arbitrator with a copy of the grievance and the company answer to it.

C. TYPES OF ARBITRATION SYSTEMS

Arbitrators can be temporary or permanent and they may be appointed singly or as part of a panel. The three most common combinations of these attributes are the single permanent arbitrator, the permanent tripartite board and the temporary arbitrator (who may sit singly or as the impartial member of a panel).

1. *The Single Permanent Arbitrator System*

Sometimes called the "Impartial Chairman" or "Umpire" system, the single permanent arbitrator system carries with it a number of significant advantages. The permanent arbitrator (who is, in reality, only "permanent" for a stated period or as long as both parties desire his continuance) possesses greater familiarity with the parties, their contract and processes, and their desires about the role of the arbitrator. This familiarity leads in turn to speedier hearings and decisions and more confidence in those decisions. There may be some disadvantages to this approach, however. The parties may choose an arbitrator only to find that he does not quite meet their expectations, and then find it difficult or awkward to dismiss him. The ready availability (and minimum fee) of a permanent arbitrator may tempt the parties to take their grievance procedure less seriously and pass on to the arbitrator cases that should be resolved between the parties themselves. It can be extremely difficult to find an experienced arbitrator with the talents and personality necessary to handle successfully the close, continuous relationship created by this system. Finally, there is a risk that the umpire may try to decide what is "good" for the parties rather than what the contract requires.

2. *The Permanent Tripartite Board*

The comments on permanency expressed above apply with equal force to the permanent tripartite board. Parties may choose the tripartite form rather than the single arbitrator to make sure their true positions (which may differ from their public positions) are forcefully presented to the neutral. This is possible because each side usually selects one member of the panel, the third member being selected by agreement, and the member selected by a side is likely to be an explicit agent of that side. In addition, the majority-vote requirement of the panel form may lend greater weight to arbitration awards. On the other hand, that same majority-vote requirement may make *any* decision hard to reach and may force the neutral to compromise his judgment to obtain the needed vote. He may wish to order reinstatement without back pay in a discharge case, for instance, but if neither of the parties is willing to compromise the neutral may be forced against his will to order back pay or to uphold the discharge. If the dissatisfied party issues a dissenting opinion, it may undercut the authority of the award and provide a rallying point for future grievances on the same issue.

3. *The Temporary Arbitrator System*

Temporary or *"ad hoc"* arbitrators are specified in most collective bargaining agreements. This system permits the parties to look for special qualifications for specialized questions and to change arbitrators easily if experience creates dissatisfaction. The temporary system does not preclude frequent or exclusive re-selection of an arbitrator who satisfies both parties, but it does eliminate some of the advantages of permanent systems.

The disadvantages of the temporary system are almost the exact opposite of the advantages of the permanent system. *Ad hoc* arbitrators will lack familiarity with the parties and their processes, will not be as consistent as a single arbitrator would (although most give some deference to prior decisions on the same issue) and may lack the necessary experience to deal with particular cases. Given these possibilities, it is likely that a losing party in one case may seek to relitigate a similar issue before a new arbitrator in hope of a better outcome, and this is not at all conducive to stable labor relations.

D. SELECTION OF THE ARBITRATOR

1. *Methods of Selection*

The ways in which parties select an arbitrator are many. Some companies and unions appoint "permanent umpires" to hear all arbitrations, either for a stated period of time or at the continued will of the parties. Some large companies and industries appoint panels of arbitrators and call upon panel members in rotation. Still others choose new arbitrators for each case by consensus, a method that has a serious disadvantage in that it does not resolve deadlocks over the choice of an individual.

Most contracts under temporary arbitrator systems specify that an arbitrator will be selected from a list of names submitted by an arbitration agency. The AAA and FMCS and several state agencies maintain files of persons qualified by education and experience to serve as arbitrators. Upon request the agency will furnish the parties with a panel of names (usually 5 or 7 in total) drawn from this list. (See Appendix 1, Form 3). The parties choose one person from the panel and then determine whether the chosen arbitrator is available for appointment.

The two most common methods for choosing one name from the panel are by alternate striking and by ranking. In the former case, the parties agree which is to strike first and then alternately eliminate the least desirable names until only one is left. Both tactical and practical reasons demand that some thought be given to the striking process at the time the arbitration clause is negotiated. Each party would like an arbitrator whose judgment, competence and prejudices it trusts, and most practitioners in the field believe that it is possible to rank each panel member with some accuracy from most to least desirable. Sophisticated lawyers therefore try to gain every possible edge in the selection process. Better knowledge of the arbitrators is one such edge, and ways to obtain such knowledge are discussed below. Effective striking is another.

Labor lawyers commonly believe that the last strike is the most important one, for it is almost the same as having the sole strike in a panel of two names. Starting with an odd number of possibilities, he who strikes first gives the even strikes, and thus the last one, to his opponent. During negotiations, therefore, the careful lawyer will try to make sure the arbitration clause gives the first strike to the other side.

Practical reasons also demand careful drafting of striking provisions. If the contract is silent, an impasse could develop over such a small matter as which party is to make the first strike. If the contract uses some such phrase as "by lot" to decide the first strike, still other questions must be answered: What method is meant by "lot"? A coin toss? Drawing straws? Who is to toss the coin or draw the straw? Does the one who "wins" the toss or draw win his choice of strikes or win the first strike?

The second method of selection eliminates some of these difficulties. Each party strikes from its own copy of the list any arbitrator deemed totally unacceptable and ranks the rest from 1 to X. The rankings of those arbitrators not eliminated by either party are then added, and the person with the lowest total is selected. If no person is left after the eliminations (a problem that could be prevented by limiting the number of strikes each party may make) another list can be obtained.

Even this method is not without some problems. What happens, for example, if two persons are tied for the lowest total ranking—if the company ranks arbitrator A first and arbitrator B second, while the union does the opposite? Perhaps the easiest way to prevent such difficulties is to incorporate by reference the rules of the AAA or FMCS, both of which provide for an appointment by the agency if for any reason the parties cannot agree upon a choice. Neither agency likes to do so, for the credibility of the arbitrator is less if the parties themselves have not selected him, but in some cases there is simply no better way.

2. *Learning About An Arbitrator*

How does a party know whether an arbitrator is "good" or "bad"? Such a judgment involves several factors, and these can be approached in different ways. The careful lawyer will want to know about the arbitrator's:

(a) *Educational Background.* Most lawyers prefer legally-trained arbitrators, believing that they will be more analytical, while many non-lawyers prefer non-lawyer arbitrators. Technical issues might call for a specialist in accounting, occupational health and safety, engineering or some other discipline.

(b) *Work Experience.* With a few exceptions, persons identified with management or labor are regarded as unlikely to be impartial, even if they have no connection with the parties in the case. Not only are management representatives likely to suspect that a union official is prejudiced (and vice-versa)—they are equally likely to regard a person with substantial experience on "their" side as untrustworthy. This is a bit subtle, but worth explaining because it helps to illustrate the careful attention serious practitioners give to the selection process.

Suppose that Doe was for many years a personnel manager for a large manufacturing company. Following his retirement he decides to use his experience in labor relations as a part-time arbitrator. A union business agent could be expected to believe that Doe has been indoctrinated for too long in the management way of thinking. But a management attorney might be equally suspicious, believing that in order to establish his credibility with union representatives Doe will have to bend over backward for unions in arbitration cases.

Arbitrators unanimously reject suggestions that they would be so mercenary—indeed, most would say that the surest way to *lose* business is to make awards based on such "political" factors —but that is nevertheless what many representatives on both sides believe. Remember, arbitration is a game of odds, and anything thought to improve those odds is likely to be used. In any event, most parties do favor arbitrators whose recent work experience has been neutral. Full-time arbitrators, academics and government officials are in the greatest demand.

(c) *Arbitration Experience.* Parties rely heavily on the length of an arbitrator's experience in arbitration, with the result that relatively few well-established arbitrators handle an extraordinary percentage of all arbitrations, and the further result that although there is much complaint about the "shortage" of qualified arbitrators it is still extremely difficult for a new person to gain a foothold in the business.

Apart from the usual benefits of experience, one reason the parties rely so heavily on experienced arbitrators is because it is easier to predict whether they will be "good" or "bad" in a particular case. An experienced arbitrator may have decided scores of discharge cases, for example, and those decisions may well give a strong hint of how he will react to the facts of a pending case.

How then do the parties learn what they need to know about an arbitrator? The arbitration agencies and the reporting services such as the

Bureau of National Affairs (BNA) and the Commerce Clearing House (CCH) provide basic biographical data but because those data are submitted by the arbitrators themselves they should be taken with a grain of salt. One professional association, the National Academy Of Arbitrators (NAA) requires substantial experience and approval of other arbitrators before a new member is admitted. Membership is no guarantee of quality, and non-membership is not an indication of lack of quality, but selection to the Academy is a favorable recommendation. BNA and CCH, among others, report a large number of arbitration awards, though nowhere near all of them. Reported cases may give some indication of experience, but those reported may be a disproportionately large or small percentage of an arbitrator's total number of decisions.

To many labor lawyers it is more important to determine an arbitrator's leanings than his experience. There are many sources for opinions on such matters. The personal experience of experienced practitioners is one important source. Many firms cross-index arbitration awards in their own cases by the arbitrator's name and thus have close at hand a sample of opinions of arbitrators in the region. Many lawyers are willing as a matter of professional courtesy to give their opinions on arbitrators they know to other attorneys on "their" side, as are company and union officials. Several private concerns, among them state and national labor organizations, chambers of commerce, employers' associations and a few for-profit companies, provide similar information.

3. *Appointment*

Where the parties are using an arbitration agency, they notify the agency of their choice and the agency then makes the formal appointment. The AAA goes one step farther than the FMCS and requires the arbitrator selected to execute a form guaranteeing his impartiality (see Appendix 2, Rule 17, and Appendix 1, Form 4.) Many parties (over 40%, by one count) select arbitrators by mutual agreement without the assistance of arbitration agencies. In such cases one or the other then calls or writes the selected arbitrator to arrange for a convenient hearing date.

E. PREPARATION FOR ARBITRATION

1. *The Grievance Procedure*

In a broad sense everything that happens between the parties beginning with the alleged breach of the agreement is in preparation for arbitration. More specifically, serious preparation begins with the grievance procedure which is usually spelled out in some detail in the agreement. Even if that procedure does not result in a settlement, it will facilitate arbitration by forcing each party to organize its own arguments and evidence and to confront those of the other side. In the process irrelevancies and inaccuracies should be weeded out with the result that, at least in theory, the arbitration hearing will be limited to relevant and relatively accurate testimony.

Contractual grievance procedures will frequently define the term "grievance." If not, the parties have little reason to interpret the term narrowly unless their contract allows all grievances to be taken to arbitration. (In that case the employer may try to limit the subjects covered by the grievance procedure to avoid the risks of arbitration). Both sides usually realize that it is better to have gripes and complaints aired in a procedure designed to correct problems than to leave them to fester in private.

Most contracts provide for a multistep grievance procedure, with three or four steps being the most common number. The grievant is usually required to bring complaints initially to his immediate supervisor in the hope that simple matters can be quickly disposed of at that level. Unresolved complaints are then taken to successively higher levels of the company hierarchy, from foreman to personnel director to plant manager, for example. If the employee had union representation at the time he presented the complaint to his supervisor, it was probably by his local union representative, the shop steward. At successive steps the grievant might be represented by the local union's business agent, the plant grievance committee, or the International Representative. Among other things, the multistep procedure encourages resolution of disputes by forcing different persons with different interests to concentrate on the issue. The system achieves its purpose well, for most grievances are resolved at an early stage and never progress to arbitration.

It is common for contracts to require that the grievance be put in writing and signed by the grievant at some early step. The requirement of a written complaint helps to focus the grievance on a specific problem, while the signature requirement is favored by employers as a way to deter frivolous grievances by making some employee take responsibility. Exceptions for matters of concern to the union as an entity or to many employees are often specified or implied so that such grievances can be processed by the union alone.

It is also common for contracts to specify time limitations on the filing and processing of grievances. Such limitations eliminate "stale" grievances and help to assure prompt resolution of fresh ones. Even when limitations are not specified, arbitrators may imply a standard of reasonableness. Of course the parties are free to waive any limitations when they believe it wise to do so. Dilatory processing of the grievance may be penalized, as by stating that the employer's last response will be deemed to settle the grievance if the union does not carry it to the next step within a certain period. Rigid adherence to such limitations may frustrate the purpose of the grievance procedure by preventing resolution of the merits of serious complaints, and it is therefore often to the advantage of both parties to waive minor lapses.

2. Preparing the Evidence

During the grievance procedure the parties will have done some preparation of the evidence and may be ready for arbitration as soon as the last step of the grievance procedure is completed. If not, they should prepare the evidence well in advance of the hearing.

The preparation required for arbitration is similar to that required for any administrative or judicial proceeding. Each party should first attempt to learn all it can about the incident giving rise to the grievance, of course. Each should study the applicable contract provisions and gather any evidence bearing upon interpretation of those provisions, such as minutes of negotiations and records of prior grievances and arbitrations. If past practice in the plant, company or industry is likely to be relevant, it too should be investigated.

Once all of the available evidence has been gathered, it must be sorted and organized. This will involve a detailed outline of the party's arguments, fleshed out by relevant evidence. It should also involve an equally detailed outline of the other party's arguments and evidence so that they can be refuted by cross-examination or presentation of appropriate evidence either in the case in chief or during rebuttal. If documentary or photographic evidence is to be used, it should be prepared so that it will be most effective upon presentation. Statistical data might be reduced to charts or graphs, for example, and photographs might be obtained to enhance the presentation of an argument.

On issues where there is no serious disagreement, the parties should consider using stipulations to conserve time and avoid confusion at the hearing (see Appendix 1, Form 7). Some evidence may not be willingly given. If that is the case, the party seeking the evidence should determine whether local law authorizes subpoenas in arbitration hearings. The proposed Uniform Arbitration Act would allow arbitrators to issue subpoenas for the attendance of witnesses and the production of evidence (see Appendix 7, Section 7), and some state laws already allow this. Other state laws allow subpoenas to be issued for arbitration by some court officer. Even in the absence of authorizing legislation, many arbitrators assume that they possess the power to order production of relevant evidence. So long as an arbitrator's order can plausibly be tied to the collective bargaining agreement or to the federal common law of labor arbitration, it is likely that such orders would be upheld by reviewing courts.

No attorney should overlook the necessity of preparing his witnesses. This does not mean that they should be told what to say; it simply means they should be helped to express clearly and forcefully what they know. At the minimum the attorney should lead the witness through his planned direct examination several times so that the questions will come as no surprise. Prudence dictates that he prepare the witness for cross-examination as well, by full discussion or perhaps by role-playing. The result should be simple, concise testimony that will hold up even under rigorous challenge.

If there is adequate time and funding available, counsel should also prepare a trial brief summarizing arguments and facts. This is a helpful way to organize one's case and if a copy is given to the arbitrator it will help him to understand that case as it is presented. (It is customary to provide a copy for the other side as well. If both parties do this, the hearing will quickly focus on the true issues in dispute).

F. THE ARBITRATION HEARING

1. *Time and Place*

According to the AAA Rules, "The Arbitrator shall fix the time and place for each hearing." (Appendix 2, Rule 19). Actually it is far more common for the parties to have a settled place for arbitrations—usually a neutral location such as a hotel, courtroom or hearing room of an impartial agency, although it may be a company or union conference room. It is also common for the parties to agree upon a few potential dates, then determine whether the arbitrator is available on one of those dates, although many leave that to the arbitrator. Once the time and place are settled, the arbitration agency will formally notify the parties and the arbitrator several days in advance (see Appendix 1, Form 5).

2. *Record of the Hearing*

Most parties take extensive notes during the hearing. One or both of the parties may want a more accurate record, however, and may arrange for a stenographer. If so, the stenographer will produce a transcript which can be referred to in briefs and in the arbitrator's opinion. If not, the arbitrator may make his own record by use of notes, shorthand, or even by a tape recorder.

3. *Swearing of the Witnesses*

The parties may agree whether witnesses are to be sworn, or may leave this decision up to the arbitrator. Under AAA Rule 24,

> The Arbitrator may, in his discretion, require witnesses to testify under oath administered by any duly qualified person, and if

required by law or requested by either party, shall do so.

Such oaths may have little legal impact (prosecutions for perjury during an arbitration are almost unheard of) but they may add dignity to the hearing and impress witnesses with the importance of telling the truth. There may be some question as to whether the arbitrator has the authority to swear in witnesses. Few statutes specifically grant the power, and unless the arbitrator is otherwise so authorized (as by being a notary public of the state in which the hearing is held) it may be necessary to call in an appropriate official. Alternatively the arbitrator may proceed even without formal authority; the psychological impact should be the same in either case.

4. *Order of Presentation*

After introductory matters such as the introduction of the arbitrator and the representatives of the parties are completed, the hearing is ready to begin. Frequently the arbitrator will begin it by reading the submission agreement or the demand and reply. His normal next step is to invite the parties to make opening statements.

At this point an interesting question arises: who is to go first? In civil and criminal trials the party bearing the burden of proof (the plaintiff or the prosecutor as the case might be) also bears the burden of going forward. This is not necessarily so in arbitration. In most cases the initiating party will be expected to go first, but in discipline and discharge cases the employer is customarily expected to begin even if the union is the initiating party. It is not clear why this should be. Some have suggested that it is because the vital facts are more likely to be in the possession of the employer, but certainly this is true of many non-discipline cases as well. Others suggest that it reflects the burden of proof, which is normally on the initiating party but is often held in discipline cases to be on the employer. Still others say that it is simply a matter of custom—that the former dean of the Yale Law School, Harry Shulman, did it that way when he was permanent umpire at Ford Motor Company in the 1940's and others have just followed his lead.

In any event the first opening statement is made, followed by a similar statement by the other party. In these statements the parties should briefly identify the issue or issues, indicate what is to be proved and (at least for the initiating party) specify the relief sought. It may be appropriate at this point in the hearing to stipulate to matters not in controversy and to introduce joint exhibits such as the contract and the documents exchanged during the grievance procedure. It is important if not essential to formulate the issue to be decided by the arbitrator before presenting the evidence on the issue. Ideally this is done by stipulation, but frequently it is necessary for the arbitrator to state his own understanding of the issue if the parties are unable to agree on the wording. The stipulated issue will be helpful in determining the relevance of offered evidence and it also delineates the arbitrator's power, for one of the few grounds for reversal of an award is a decision that goes beyond the scope of the stipulated issue.

Thereafter the arbitration hearing normally proceeds like a trial:

(a) Presentation of witnesses by the party going first, with opportunity for cross-examination after the direct examination.

(b) Presentation of witnesses by the other party, with like opportunity for cross-examination.

(c) Rebuttal witnesses, if appropriate.

(d) Summation by both parties.

Documentary and other evidence should be properly identified and authenticated by a witness and presented to the arbitrator with a copy to the other side. At some point in the hearing it may be appropriate for the arbitrator and the parties to leave the hearing room to examine evidence that cannot be brought into it—a machine in an automation case or a work process in a staffing dispute, for example. If this is seen to be likely, plans should be made in advance and the inspection scheduled at the point of the hearing at which it is most relevant.

This describes the customary hearing procedure. Because it is customary it may be altered by the arbitrator or the parties. In every case some structure should be retained to avoid confusion but in no case should a degree of formality be imposed that would prevent a complete airing of the dispute. Arbitration has therapeutic values beyond the mere fact of a decision, and an overly technical application of procedural rules may make that therapy ineffective.

5. Briefs

The parties may choose to submit written briefs in lieu of or in addition to closing arguments. This is particularly helpful to the arbitrator in complicated cases, but briefs should not be used to present new evidence or theories. If briefs are to be submitted or a transcript prepared the arbitrator will set agreeable time limits and will not formally close the hearing until the briefs and transcript are received. Otherwise the hearing will be closed after the summations of the parties.

6. The Award

Unless the parties agree otherwise, AAA Rules oblige the arbitrator to render his award within 30 days of the closing of the hearing (Appendix 2,

Rule 37), and FMCS regulations encourage an award within 60 days (Appendix 4, Section 1404.-15(a)). Usually the award will be accompanied by an opinion setting forth the reasons for the award. Unless state law or the relevant contract provides otherwise, the authority of the arbitrator ends with the issuance of the award. An award may not be changed by the arbitrator unless the parties agree to reopen the proceeding and restore the power of the arbitrator. Failing such agreement the only recourse of a dissatisfied party is to the courts.

7. *Costs*

Arbitration is supposed to be a relatively inexpensive alternative to a law suit. It may in fact be less expensive but as the procedure has become more formal in recent years, involving lawyers and a stenographer as well as an arbitrator, costs have increased remarkably. A party contemplating arbitration should weigh potential gains against the following:

(a) The time and expenses of participants. If a party chooses to be represented by an attorney, costs rise significantly. Investigation of the facts, presentation of exhibits and writing of briefs may cost a considerable amount.

(b) Cost of the stenographic record.

(c) Fee and expenses of the arbitrator.

[*33*]

(d) Administrative fee of the arbitration association.

(e) Rental of the hearing room.

Parties may be able to economize on several items, as by dispensing with briefs and transcript and holding the hearing in a location owned by one of the parties. Other expenses are usually shared equally (administrative costs and arbitrator's fee and expenses) or borne exclusively by the party incurring them (one's own time, expenses and attorney's fees).

III

THE LEGAL STATUS OF LABOR ARBITRATION

A. AT COMMON LAW

Until very recent times courts in the United States have not been receptive to labor arbitration. This critical attitude seems to have been due chiefly to matters beyond the merits or demerits of labor arbitration itself. The courts faced an initial difficulty in dealing with arbitration clauses in collective agreements because one party to the contract, the union, was an unincorporated association. In many jurisdictions, therefore, a union could not sue or be sued as an entity.

A second difficulty involved the nature of collective agreements. Strictly speaking, they are not contracts at all, for only in individual contracts of employment, express or implied, is consideration (the offer of work and the promise to do it) exchanged. In Great Britain this is still the law, but in the United States a number of courts gave practical effect to labor agreements by treating them either as stating a "custom" or "usage" which is reflected in each individual contract of employment, or by treating the union as an "agent" of its members, or by regarding individual employees as third party beneficiaries of the contract between the union and the employer. Even if collective agreements were treated as contracts, executory agreements to arbitrate were deemed revocable at any time by either party.

A third difficulty was the jealousy of courts of equity to all forms of arbitration. Agreements to arbitrate were viewed by those courts as attempts to "oust them from their jurisdiction" and were therefore denied specific enforcement. An action could still be brought at law for breach of contract, but because of the difficulty of proving actual harm only nominal damages were available in the typical case.

Because of these difficulties, statutes were thought necessary to make effective arbitration possible. There were several of these, beginning in the nineteenth century.

B. STATUTES BEFORE THE TAFT–HARTLEY ACT

1. *Early State Laws on Arbitration*

By 1886, at least eight states had adopted statutes providing either for *ad hoc* arbitration boards, usually appointed by district courts, or for permanent, full-time state boards of arbitration. The idea caught on, and sixteen more states enacted legislation by 1901. Only four states had more than ten cases before 1904 or so, however, and except in Massachusetts most of the cases handled involved mediation rather than arbitration as we know it today.

2. *Federal Legislation for Railway Labor Disputes*

Early federal legislation for the settlement of railway labor disputes was no more effective than the early state statutes. Congress passed the Arbitration Act of 1888, which provided for mediation and for voluntary arbitration before neutral *ad hoc* arbitration boards, but those provisions were not used a single time during the ten years the Act was in force. The Erdman Act of 1898 also provided for mediation and for voluntary arbitration, but specified that the arbitration board would consist of a representative of each side and a third person agreed upon by those representatives or, in the event they could not agree, appointed by federal officials. The Erdman Act was not used at all until 1906, but from that year until 1912 there were twelve cases of settlement by arbitration. The Newlands Act of 1913 established a new government agency to deal with railway disputes, the Board of Mediation and Conciliation. In its thirteen year existence the Board helped to settle twenty-one cases by arbitration. After the failure of the Transportation Act of 1920, which set up a tripartite Railway Labor Board with arbitration authority but no enforcement power, Congress passed the Railway Labor Act of 1926, which, as amended, still governs the settlement of labor disputes in that industry. Under that law grievance disputes are brought before one of four divisions of the National Railway Adjustment Board which is composed of equal numbers of labor and management representatives. In the case of a tie vote, the decision is left to a neutral referee. The RLA dispute resolution procedures have been used in tens of thousands of cases. Neither side has been completely satisfied with them —employers complain of too many union victories and unions complain of lengthy procedural delays —but they do seem to be a substantial improvement over those in earlier laws.

3. Other Federal Laws Before 1947

The two World Wars made quick settlement of labor disputes essential. The Wilson administration in World War I took the position that all labor disputes in war industries should be arbitrated, but never sought legislation making arbitration compulsory. A number of new tripartite labor dispute adjustment agencies were established, however, and many of these did engage in *de facto* arbitration enforced by indirect means of compulsion when mediation efforts failed. The most important of these agencies was the National War Labor Board which was in existence during the last year of the First World War and served as a model for a similar board in the next war.

Perhaps the greatest impetus to labor arbitration in the twentieth century was the War Labor Board established during World War II by President Franklin Roosevelt. The impact of the War Labor Board was three-fold: (a) it arbitrated thousands of labor disputes directly; (b) it frequently used its power to resolve negotiation disputes to insert grievance arbitration clauses in collective bargaining agreements (these clauses encouraged non-governmental arbitration, and the experiences of labor and management were favorable enough to recommend the process to them after the War); and (c) it provided a corps of experienced professional arbitrators, many of whom are still active today.

One other federal statute deserves mention. In 1925 Congress passed the United States Arbitration Act (Appendix 6) which made arbitration agreements in contracts involving interstate or international commerce specifically enforceable. That law excludes "contracts of employment" but there is some dispute as to whether the exclusion applies only to individual contracts or also to collective agreements. Lower federal court decisions on the question are in conflict, and the Supreme Court has not clearly spoken to the issue. Justice Frankfurter, dissenting in the *Lincoln Mills* case discussed below, construed the majority opinion in that case as a silent rejection of the applicability of this act to labor disputes, but his view has not been widely accepted. Nevertheless that decision did provide alternate grounds for federal court action and thus made use of the United States Arbitration Act unnecessary in most cases.

4. *Modern State Arbitration Laws*

There have been two major attempts to draft a uniform state arbitration act that would gain wide acceptance. The first attempt, in 1925, was a failure and the proposal was withdrawn after adoption by a few states. The second attempt produced the Uniform Arbitration Act (see Appendix 7). The National Conference of Commissioners on Uniform State Laws approved the draft in 1955 and recommended enactment in all states. Fewer than twenty have enacted anything close to the Uniform Act, and several of those did so only after eliminating collective bargaining agreements from coverage.

Most of the major industrial states do have arbitration statutes applicable to labor disputes. Some of these merely charge a state agency to "promote" arbitration and others were designed primarily for commercial disputes, but many are detailed laws clearly envisioning labor arbitration. Among the states having comprehensive laws are California, Illinois, Massachusetts, Michigan, New Jersey, New York, and Ohio. Most of these statutes follow similar lines. They generally provide for state court enforcement of labor arbitration agreements and supervision of the process, a formal hearing, issuance of subpoenae, and judicial review and enforcement of awards.

The relationship between state statutes governing labor arbitration and federal labor relations law is far from settled. As will be seen in the following pages, federal law recognizes that state statutes and courts are relevant to labor arbitration under the Labor-Management Relations Act, but state laws must be consistent with the federal policy. The difficulty in applying this general rule of accommodation is that almost any provision of state law affecting arbitration can be interpreted by one party as interfering with federal policy. A grant of subpoena power to arbitrators might be viewed as a means of improving the quality or quantity of evidence on which the arbitrator will make his decision, but the recipient of the subpoena might just as easily regard it as an unwarranted intrusion into matters best left to collective bargaining, an intrusion that actually hinders arbitration agreements by making them less attractive to potential subpoena recipients.

There has been little litigation on this question, but those few courts to have dealt with the issue seem to treat state laws as valid *prima facie,* that is, until clearly shown to be in conflict with some aspect of federal policy. In one notable case, a federal appeals court held that a state law requiring arbitration awards to be issued within a stated time could not be used to challenge a late award. *West Rock Lodge No. 2120, IAM v. Geometric Tool Co.,* 406 F.2d 284 (2d Cir. 1968).

C. SECTION 301 OF THE TAFT-HARTLEY ACT

1. The Language of Section 301

In the Labor-Management Relations Act of 1947 (LMRA, more commonly known as the Taft-Hartley Act) Congress stated its preference for arbitration by declaring in Section 203(d) that "Final adjustment by a method agreed upon by the parties" is "the desirable method for settlement of grievance disputes."

Of far greater importance for labor arbitration is Section 301 of that Act. Because that Section has been so important, it is worthwhile to examine it in some detail. The first two subsections, the most important for our purposes, read:

SUITS BY AND AGAINST LABOR ORGANIZATIONS

SEC. 301(a) Suits for violation of contracts between an employer and a labor organization representing employees in an industry affecting commerce as defined in this Act, or between any such labor organizations, may be brought in any district court of the United States having jurisdiction of the parties, without respect to the amount in controversy or without regard to the citizenship of the parties.

(b) Any labor organization which represents employees in an industry affecting commerce as defined in this Act and any employer whose activities affect commerce as defined in this Act shall be bound by the acts of its agents. Any such labor organization may sue or be sued as an entity and in behalf of the employees whom it represents in the courts of the United States. Any money judgment against a labor organization in a district court of the United States shall be enforceable only against the organization as an entity and against its assets, and shall not be enforceable against any individual member or his assets.

Some of the effects of this section should be clear from the language. Among other things, it eliminated some of the hindrances to common law suits to enforce arbitration agreements by allowing a union to sue and be sued as an entity and by clearly stating that collective bargaining agreements are enforceable contracts. Other effects became clear only after many years of litigation.

2. The "Lincoln Mills" Case

After enactment of Section 301 there was a great deal of debate over whether that section gave federal courts authority to compel or stay arbitration or to enforce or vacate arbitration awards, and if so, what substantive law was to be applied in such actions. The primary question at issue in *Textile Workers Union v. Lincoln Mills of Alabama,* 353 U.S. 448 (1957), an action to force a reluctant employer to abide by a promise to arbitrate certain grievances, was whether Section 301 was simply **jurisdictional** (that is, whether it gave the federal courts jurisdiction over the parties but left applicable state substantive law intact), or **substantive** as well (that is, whether the federal courts were to apply a new federal law in the exercise of their jurisdiction). In an opinion by Justice Douglas the Court left no doubt where it stood on this issue. It held, first, that Congress authorized specific performance of promises to arbitrate grievances, and second, that "the substantive law to apply in suits under § 301(a) is federal law, which the courts must fashion from the policy of our national labor laws." State law may be relevant in the fashioning of that law, the Court said, but "Any state law applied . . . will be absorbed as federal law and will not be an independent source of private rights." Finally, the Court rejected the argument that the anti-injunction policy of the Norris-LaGuardia Act prohibited specific enforcement, for "the failure to arbitrate was not a part and parcel of the abuses against which the Act was aimed." Norris-La-

Guardia, in other words, was to be read in conjunction with the pro-arbitration policy of the Taft-Hartley Act, not in opposition to it.

Subsequent cases have expanded the impact of *Lincoln Mills*. In *Charles Dowd Box Co. v. Courtney*, 368 U.S. 502 (1962) and *Local 174, Teamsters v. Lucas Flour Co.*, 369 U.S. 95 (1962) the Supreme Court held that state courts retained concurrent jurisdiction to enforce collective bargaining agreements but that in doing so they must apply federal law fashioned in light of *Lincoln Mills*. One other part of the *Lucas Flour* decision is at least tangentially relevant here. Operating on the assumption that arbitration is a *quid pro quo* for agreements not to strike, the court held that a no-strike promise should be implied in any dispute "which a collective bargaining agreement provides shall be settled exclusively and finally by compulsory arbitration." Other cases have given the federal courts power to compel a successor employer to abide by an arbitration agreement made by his predecessor, to grant judgments where the right or duty to arbitrate is not clear, and to enjoin strikes in cases covered by mandatory arbitration provisions.

3. *An Introduction to the Relationship Between the Arbitrator and the Courts: The "Steelworkers Trilogy"*

In a 1960 trio of cases, the *"Steelworkers Trilogy,"* the Supreme Court addressed the problem of the relationship between arbitral and judicial processes. In what seemed to many observers to be an extraordinary exercise in judicial abnegation, the Court, speaking again through Justice Douglas, clearly placed arbitration in the dominant position. In fairness to the Court it should be pointed out that in order to establish the primacy of arbitration under federal labor policy the Court had to overcome several decades of judicial coolness toward that procedure, and this may have caused Justice Douglas to overstate his case.

Typical of the prior judicial attitude is a decision explicitly criticized in the *Trilogy*, *International Ass'n of Machinists v. Cutler-Hammer, Inc.*, 271 App.Div. 917, 67 N.Y.S.2d 317 (1947), aff'd 297 N.Y. 519, 74 N.E.2d 464 (1947). The contract at issue in that case provided that "the Company agrees to meet with the Union early in July 1946 to discuss payment of a bonus for the first six months of 1946" and that the parties would arbitrate disputes as to the "meaning, performance, non-performance or application" of its provisions. A meeting was held at which the parties discussed *whether* a bonus was to be paid. The union took the position that the contract meant that a bonus *must* be paid and that all there was to discuss was the amount of the bonus. When the employer refused to pay a bonus, the union demanded arbitration and sought a court order to compel it. The New York court denied the union's request, stating that "If the meaning of the provision of the contract sought to be arbitrated is beyond dispute, there cannot be anything to arbitrate and the contract cannot be said to provide for arbitration" and holding that this contract required only discussion. The union's demand for actual payment was therefore not within the scope of the arbitration clause. As will be seen, the Supreme Court expressly rejected the *Cutler-Hammer* approach.

The first two cases of the *Steelworkers Trilogy* involved union attempts in Section 301 actions to force reluctant employers into arbitration. *United Steelworkers v. American Mfg. Co.*, 363 U.S. 564 (1960), involved a claim the employer felt was not arbitrable. One Sparks, an employee of the respondent, left his work due to an injury and brought an action for compensation benefits. That action was settled on the basis of a permanent partial disability, but two weeks later the union filed a grievance charging that Sparks was entitled to return to his job. The employer refused to arbitrate the grievance and its refusal was upheld by the lower federal courts, the district court applying an estoppel theory because Sparks had settled the compensation case on the basis of a permanent disability and the circuit court stating that the grievance was "a frivolous, patently baseless one, not subject to arbitration under the collective bargaining agreement."

The Supreme Court reversed, holding that the agreement (which contained a standard arbitration clause providing arbitration for all disputes "as to the meaning, interpretation and application of the provisions of this agreement") was to submit *all* grievances to arbitration, "not merely those that a court may deem to be meritorious." The function of a court in such cases is very limited:

> It is confined to ascertaining whether the party seeking arbitration is making a claim which on its face is governed by the contract. Whether the moving party is right or wrong is a question of contract interpretation for the arbitrator.

This is so, said the Court, both because of the national labor policy favoring arbitration and because "The processing of even frivolous claims may have therapeutic values of which those who are not a part of the plant environment may be quite unaware."

United Steelworkers of America v. Warrior and Gulf Navigation Co., 363 U.S. 574 (1960), involved a similarly broad arbitration clause, but the contract in that case also provided that "matters which are strictly a function of management shall not be subject to arbitration." The union sought a court order forcing arbitration of its claim that the employer violated the agreement by contracting out certain work. The lower federal courts dismissed the complaint, agreeing with the employer that contracting out fell within the exception for "matters which are strictly a function of management."

Again the Supreme Court reversed. There is no room under federal labor policy for the hostility toward arbitration the courts have shown in commercial cases, said the Court. To the contrary, since arbitration in these cases is a substitute for labor strife rather than for litigation the courts should read arbitration clauses in the manner most favorable to arbitration:

> An order to arbitrate the particular grievance should not be denied unless it may be said with positive assurance that the arbitration clause is not susceptible of an interpretation that covers the asserted dispute. Doubts should be resolved in favor of coverage.

Why should such matters of interpretation be left to arbitrators rather than the courts? Because the parties want them to be, answered Justice Douglas. The collective bargaining agreement is part of an attempt to establish a system of industrial self-government, the gaps in which "may be left to be filled in by reference to the practices of the particular industry and of the various shops covered by the agreement." The labor arbitrator is selected for his knowledge of "the common law of the shop" and for his ability to bring to bear considerations which "may indeed be foreign to the competence of courts. . . . The ablest judge cannot be expected to bring the same experience and competence to bear upon the determination of a grievance, because he cannot be similarly informed."

Moreover, Justice Douglas went on, because a no-strike clause is the usual trade-off for an arbitration agreement, an absolute no-strike clause (as was present in this case) subjects "in a very real sense" everything management does to the arbitration clause. Any exceptions must be explicit, and the phrase "strictly a function of management" does not explicitly cover contracting out.

Warrior & Gulf does not mean that all questions of arbitrability are for the courts to decide. The parties can of course specify that issues of substantive arbitrability are themselves matters for the arbitrator, and in a later case, *John Wiley & Sons, Inc. v. Livingston,* 376 U.S. 543 (1964), the Court held that issues of "procedural arbitrability"—*i. e.,* compliance with procedural conditions established in the contract—are to be resolved by the arbitrator. It does mean, though, that unless otherwise specified the courts are to resolve questions of substantive arbitrability, and resolve them in favor of arbitration whenever possible.

The third case, *United Steelworkers of America v. Enterprise Wheel & Car Corp.,* 363 U.S. 593 (1960), looked at the relationship between the arbitrator and the courts from a different perspective. There the issue was not whether arbitration agreements should be specifically enforced, but whether arbitration awards rendered pursuant to such agreements should be enforced. In other words, are the courts any freer to interpret the meaning of the contract after the arbitrator has spoken than before? The dispute involved an arbitration award requiring reinstatement of discharged employees with backpay even for a period following the termination date of the contract. The circuit court of appeals refused to enforce the portion of the award granting reinstatement and backpay beyond the contract termination date.

Once again the Supreme Court reversed, holding that the policy of judicial deference to arbitration was appropriate after issuance of the award as well as before. If courts had the final say on the merits of arbitration awards the federal policy favoring voluntary arbitration would be undermined. This is not to say that the arbitrator can do entirely as he wishes; he "does not sit to dispense his own brand of industrial justice." Rather, his award is legitimate "only so long as it draws its essence from the collective bargaining agreement." He may look for guidance from

[*51*]

many sources, need not provide reasons for the award, and should not be overruled because of an ambiguity in the opinion "which permits the inference that the arbitrator may have exceeded his authority"—but where it is clear that the arbitrator's words "manifest an infidelity to this obligation," the court must refuse to enforce the award. In this case, however, no such infidelity was evident, and the court below was wrong to substitute its judgment on the merits for that of the arbitrator.

Justice Douglas' discovery of a federal policy heavily weighted in favor of arbitration and his unbounded praise of arbitrators and the arbitration process have not gone unchallenged. Justice Whittaker, dissenting in *Warrier & Gulf,* termed the assertion that federal policy grants arbitrators powers far beyond the contract and (when there is a no-strike clause) makes everything that management does subject to arbitration "an entirely new and strange doctrine," for which the Court cited no legislative or judicial authority. A few years later a distinguished arbitrator and federal judge, Paul Hays, endorsed Whittaker's criticisms and carried them even further. In the Storrs Lectures on Jurisprudence at Yale Law School, later published as *Labor Arbitration: A Dissenting View* (1966), Hays challenged the core of Douglas' position, that arbitrators are better qualified in this field than "the ablest judge."

"No authority whatever is cited for any of these statements," says Hays, and "I know of no authority that would lend them support." An arbitrator is chosen because the parties believe he will render a favorable verdict or because of a perceived ability to interpret the written agreement, not because of any trust in his judgment about considerations not expressed in the contract. In other words, they choose arbitrators for the same skills a judge would use—and if this is so, there is no reason to give arbitration a position of such dominance.

Such criticisms have not done much to change the attitude of the courts. With only rare exceptions the courts have to this day been almost as respectful of arbitration as Justice Douglas was in the *Steelworkers Trilogy*. One result of the Court's approach has been to enhance the finality of arbitrators' decisions by making review on the merits practically unobtainable. In general the *Trilogy* has kept arbitration disputes out of the courts.

4. *Section 301 and the Norris-LaGuardia Act: Boys Markets and After*

If there has been a single preeminent rule of federal labor policy in the past half-century, it is that the federal courts ought not to use their injunctive power to break strikes. Implicitly the Clayton Anti-Trust Act (1914) and explicitly the

Norris-LaGuardia Act (1932) limited the federal courts in this regard. It was inevitable that some newer but equally important policy would eventually come into conflict with the anti-injunction rule. That finally happened in *Boys Markets, Inc. v. Retail Clerks Local 770,* 398 U.S. 235 (1970), where the anti-injunction rule was forced to bow to the pro-arbitration policy enunciated 10 years earlier in the *Trilogy.*

The stage for that ruling was set by several Supreme Court decisions in the years following the *Trilogy. Dowd Box v. Courtney,* 368 U.S. 502 (1962), held that state courts had concurrent jurisdiction with the federal courts over Section 301 suits to enforce collective bargaining agreements. In doing so state courts would have to apply federal substantive law, *Local 174, Teamsters v. Lucas Flour Co.,* 369 U.S. 95 (1962), but they would presumably retain their own procedural and remedial law. The catch to this was that state courts were not bound by the Norris-LaGuardia Act, and at least some jurisdictions allowed specific enforcement of no-strike clauses. In other words it would be possible for state courts, exercising jurisdiction under a federal statute and applying federal substantive principles, to do something federal courts had been prohibited from doing for several decades, that is, enjoin strikes.

This would have been clear enough but for one complicating problem. In *Avco Corp. v. IAM Lodge 735,* 390 U.S. 557 (1968), the Supreme Court held that a union sued in a state court for breach of a no-strike clause and thus potentially subject to an injunction could remove the case to the federal courts. The federal courts were prohibited from issuing an injunction in such cases by an earlier decision of the Supreme Court, *Sinclair Refining Co. v. Atkinson,* 370 U.S. 195 (1962).

Something had to give. It was clearly inconsistent to hold that Congress intended in Section 301 to supplement rather than displace state court jurisdiction in these cases, which the Court did in *Dowd Box,* and yet allow a *de facto* displacement of state injunctive power by unlimited removal to federal courts which could not grant injunctive relief, which was of course the practical effect of *Avco* and *Sinclair*.

Sinclair gave. A new majority of the Court, stating that it was simply accommodating the Norris-LaGuardia Act to the new legislation favoring peaceful resolution of labor disputes, held in *Boys Markets* that in certain cases the federal courts could enjoin a strike in breach of a no-strike clause. The holding was a narrow one, applying only where the contract agreed to by the union contained a mandatory grievance adjustment or arbitration procedure, and not always even then.

Quoting from the dissenting opinion in *Sinclair,* the Court adopted some rather severe limiting principles:

> A District Court entertaining an action under § 301 may not grant injunctive relief against concerted activity unless and until it decides that the case is one in which an injunction would be appropriate despite the Norris-La-Guardia Act. When a strike is sought to be enjoined because it is over a grievance which both parties are contractually bound to arbitrate, the District Court may issue no injunctive order until it first holds that the contract *does* have that effect; and the employer should be ordered to arbitrate, as a condition of his obtaining an injunction against the strike. Beyond this, the District Court must, of course, consider whether issuance of an injunction would be warranted under ordinary principles of equity—whether breaches are occurring and will continue, or have been threatened and will be committed; whether they have caused or will cause irreparable injury to the employer; and whether the employer will suffer more from the denial of an injunction than will the union from its issuance.

To reiterate, *Boys Markets* sets forth three tests for a strike injunction: the strike must be over a grievance which the parties are contractually bound to arbitrate; the employer must be ordered to arbitrate, as well as the union; and traditional equity principles must be satisfied. The last two of these are self-explanatory, but the first deserves some explanation.

The strike must be "over a grievance which both parties are contractually bound to arbitrate." Note that there is no requirement of an express no-strike clause. In *Lucas Flour* the Court, over the bitter dissent of Justice Black, held that a broad mandatory arbitration clause implies a no-strike obligation and more recently, in *Gateway Coal Co. v. UMW,* 414 U.S. 368 (1974), the Court allowed enforcement of such a "constructive no-strike agreement" by injunction.

Note, too, that the strike must be over an arbitrable grievance. What happens where the strike itself, not the underlying cause, is the alleged violation of the contract subject to arbitration? That was precisely the issue in *Buffalo Forge Co. v. United Steelworkers,* 428 U.S. 397 (1976). The union was the representative of three groups of employees of the same employer. While the union was negotiating a contract for one of these groups, it was party to collective bargaining agreements for the other two, and both of those agreements contained arbitration and no-strike provisions. The first group (clerical and technical employees) struck when negotiations failed and after a few days the union ordered the others (production and maintenance workers) to honor the picket lines of the first.

The underlying cause of the strike by the production and maintenance workers was the failure of negotiations involving the clerical and technical workers, and that failure could hardly be the subject of a grievance under the existing contracts governing production and maintenance employees. Moreover, although the employer was willing to go to arbitration the strike itself would be the arbitrable issue, not some motivating cause. In a 5–4 decision the Supreme Court held that *Boys Markets* did not authorize injunctions against sympathy strikes. Speaking for the Court, Justice White said that the "driving force" of the earlier decision was the strong congressional preference for the private dispute settlement mechanisms agreed upon by the parties; strikes over arbitrable issues would of course frustrate such arbitral processes and deprive the employer of the *quid pro quo* for his promise to arbitrate. That was not the case in *Buffalo Forge,* said Justice White, for a strike over a non-arbitrable issue neither frustrates the arbitration process nor deprives the employer of the benefit of his bargain. As a result it is not necessary in such cases to accommodate the Norris-LaGuardia Act to Section 301, and the sole admittedly arbitrable issue, the permissibility of the sympathy strike under the terms of the collective bargaining agreements, must itself be decided by the arbitrator before an injunction would be appropriate. (The union here did not refuse to go to arbitration. If it had refused, presumably it could have been required to arbitrate pursuant to *Lincoln Mills*).

The attentive reader may perceive some inconsistency between *Boys Markets* and *Buffalo Forge*. If the reasons for allowing any exceptions to the Norris-LaGuardia Act's prohibitions on strike injunctions were to promote the arbitration process and guarantee the employer his *quid* (uninterrupted production during the term of the agreement) for his *quo* (his agreement to arbitrate disputes), then surely these same policies call for enjoining sympathy strikes as well as others. The facts of the case give no reason to believe the parties had intended their no-strike clause to be so limited, and the possibility of judicial error in granting injunctions is no greater where only one issue (the strike itself) is to be submitted to arbitration rather than two (the strike itself and the underlying cause).

Moreover, the possible ramifications of *Buffalo Forge* reach far beyond the sympathy strike situation. If injunctions are inappropriate unless the strike is over an arbitrable issue, then a wide range of strikes which are clearly in breach of an agreement may not be halted by the courts even for the period during which a grievance is pending before an arbitrator. Among these would be strikes over other non-arbitrable issues such as an employer's pricing, advertising or marketing practices, or his dealings with other companies or governments opposed by the union; strikes to change the terms of a contract during the contract term; and strikes over no issue at all, as occasionally seems to be the case in coal-mine wildcats. However flagrantly such strikes might violate the union's own agreement, however seriously they might interfere with production, they may not be enjoined because of the *Buffalo Forge* decision.

One last aspect of the sympathy strike problem should be mentioned. Suppose the grievance underlying the **primary** strike is arbitrable (unlike the *Buffalo Forge* situation, where the cause of the strike was the failure of contract negotiations, a non-arbitrable issue), but only under the contract of the primary union. This obviously falls somewhere between the *Boys Markets* and *Buffalo Forge* situations, and the courts have not had an easy time dealing with it. In the leading case of *Cedar Coal Co. v. UMW Local 1759,* 560 F.2d 1153 (4th Cir. 1977), cert. denied 434 U.S. 1047 (1978), the court faced just this problem and struck a new balance, holding that when the purpose and potential effect of a sympathy strike are to compel the primary strikers' employer to concede an arbitrable issue to the striking union, an injunction may be issued against the sympathy strike as well as the primary strike. In the *Cedar Coal* case the employer, collective bargaining agreement, bargaining unit and locality of employment were the same as to both unions, which were different locals of the same international. Whether the "object of the strike" test will be applied in different circumstances is impossible to predict. Indeed, the *Cedar Coal* court refused to apply its own test to a third local whose members were employed by a different employer.

IV

ARBITRATION, THE NLRB, AND THE COURTS

This chapter will discuss in greater detail a number of the issues mentioned briefly in the preceding pages. In addition it will deal with several new issues, among them the attitude of the NLRB toward labor arbitration, the role the NLRB plays in unfair labor practice disputes that also involve labor arbitration, and how arbitrators react to potential conflicts between the contract they are interpreting and the formal law.

A. ARBITRABILITY

Arbitrability—that is, the question whether a particular dispute is properly subject to arbitration—has two aspects. A claim is sometimes made that the subject matter of a grievance is not arbitrable because there is no valid contract in force, because the contract does not deal with certain issues or the arbitration clause does not seem to include them, or because specific exclusions from the contract or the arbitration clause prohibit arbitration. These types of objections refer to **substantive arbitrability**. Another category of objections involves claims that procedural requisites to arbitration have not been met. This category deals with **procedural arbitrability** and includes, among other things, arguments that there is not a proper grievant or that time limitations or other specified formalities have not been complied with.

1. *Substantive Arbitrability*

The Supreme Court in the *Steelworkers Trilogy* severely restricted the role courts were to play in determinations of substantive arbitrability. When a party brings a case before the court seeking to force or block arbitration, the court is confined "to ascertaining whether the party seeking arbitration is making a claim which on its face is governed by the contract" (*American Mfg. Co.*). In making even that determination, the court must order arbitration "unless it may be said with positive assurance that the arbitration clause is not susceptible of an interpretation that covers the dispute." Doubts are to be resolved in favor of coverage (*Warrior & Gulf Nav. Co.*). Only an express exclusion or "the most forceful evidence" of a purpose to exclude a claim from arbitration can prevail against this pro-arbitration policy. Once the arbitrator renders his award, the courts may not tamper with it so long as it "draws its essence from the collective bargaining agreement," which means the written contract and any additions to it by virtue of past practice (*Enterprise Wheel & Car Corp.*).

Notwithstanding these strictures, many courts have found themselves dealing with questions of substantive arbitrability rather more deeply than the language of the *Trilogy* would seem to allow. Indeed, the Supreme Court itself provided one way for this to happen when, in *John Wiley & Sons v. Livingston*, 376 U.S. 543 (1964), it recognized that at some point the demand for arbitration might be "so plainly unreasonable that the subject matter of the dispute must be regarded as non-arbitrable because it can be seen in advance that no award to the Union can receive judicial sanction." The difficulty with making such a determination is that it necessitates a review of the evidence on the merits of a case, if not a judgment thereon, and the *Trilogy* seemed to warn the courts against making such a review.

In order for a subject to be arbitrable under a contract, there must of course be a contract in effect. Thus a grievance which arises after a contract terminates is not subject to the expired arbitration clause. If the grievance involves rights that may have "vested" during the term of the contract, or if arbitration has been initiated prior to the expiration of the contract, the arbitrator is not deprived of his jurisdiction by the expiration. He may, on the merits, lack the authority to rule in favor of the claimant, however. In *John Wiley & Sons, supra,* the Supreme Court held that a merged employer was bound to arbitrate with a union that represented employees of one of the predecessor companies, even though the contract between that company and the union had expired, for the union claimed that certain rights had vested and that arbitration was the method provided in the contract to resolve such disputes. When the arbitrator heard the case on the merits, however, he held that the rights claimed by the union expired with the rest of the contract. *Interscience Encyclopedia, Inc.,* 55 LA 210 (B. Roberts, 1970).

Occasionally the courts will find a particular claim to be non-arbitrable simply because the contract is silent on the issue, as the Seventh Circuit did in *Independent Petroleum Workers of America, Inc. v. American Oil Co.,* 324 F.2d 903 (7th Cir. 1963), aff'd by an equally divided court, 379 U.S. 130 (1964), where the union unsuccessfully sought arbitration of a subcontracting dispute. The agreement contained a standard arbitration clause but no reference to subcontracting, and according to the circuit court the bargaining history of the parties showed that the union had tried but failed to limit the company's right to contract out work. That decision probably represents a minority position, for most courts, when faced with a broad arbitration clause and no other specific reference to the disputed issue, would order arbitration simply because of the possibility that the agreement may have been tacitly amended by past practice or that other clauses (recognition, seniority, etc.) might have been intended to cover the issue.

The courts have not welcomed the notion of implied exclusions. A common management rights clause giving the employer the "exclusive right" to make certain decisions will not prevent arbitration of a grievance challenging one of those decisions, for example, absent a further statement in the contract that the exercise of that right shall be non-arbitrable. *United Ins. Co. v. Insurance Workers Int'l Union,* 315 F.Supp. 1133 (E.D.Pa. 1970). The attempted exclusion in that case, if that is what it was, was not explicit, nor did the employer show "the most forceful evidence" of an intent to exclude that subject.

It is more common for the courts to rule against substantive arbitrability where the contract contains a specific exclusion, a possibility the Supreme Court recognized in *Warrior & Gulf* but limited there to clear, unambiguous exclusions. Most courts take the view that general language limiting arbitration, such as common prohibitions on arbitrators modifying or adding to the contract, affect only the arbitrator's "authority" to render a particular award, not to his "jurisdiction" to hear the case. This attitude seems to stem from the "therapeutic" value of arbitration the Supreme Court recognized in *Trilogy*. The parties may benefit from the decision of an outsider, even where the contract gives the outsider only a single choice.

The tighter the parties make the language of the arbitration clause, the greater the chance that a court will refuse to order arbitration. The odds of that happening go up significantly, for example, where the contract provides for arbitration only where the union can allege a violation of a specific clause, and the odds go down significantly where the contract provides for arbitration of "any dispute."

Similarly, exclusion of a specific subject from arbitration is likely to be enforced by the courts. In a case reaching the Second Circuit, for example, the agreement said that "in no event" shall a dispute arising out of the promotion clause "be subject to arbitration." The union nevertheless sought to force arbitration of a promotion dispute, but was turned down because not even the strong presumption in favor of arbitration could overcome such clear language. *Communications Workers v. New York Tel. Co.,* 327 F.2d 94 (2d Cir. 1964).

Suppose that a court orders arbitration of a dispute where one party claims the matter is not arbitrable. May the arbitrator then decide the contrary? Some of the language of the *Trilogy* seems to prohibit such a redetermination. The pro-arbitration presumption enunciated in those cases might be equally binding upon arbitrators, and although the Court in *Warrior & Gulf* recognized that the parties could agree to leave arbitrability questions to the arbitrator it held that the party claiming that to be the case "must bear the burden of a clear demonstration of that purpose." Both fairness to the parties and the underlying principle of the *Trilogy* would allow the arbitrator to make a new decision, however. The courts, after all, are told only to make the most superficial investigation, to ask only whether the contract "on its face" governs the issue. To prohibit the arbitrator, too, from looking deeper into the question would deprive the parties of the only other forum available for determining their true intent. It would amount to a requirement that on the question of arbitrability all decision-makers are to make only a superficial determination (and a biased one at that, for all doubts are to be resolved in favor of arbitration) and none would be allowed to determine what the parties really meant. This would indeed be a strange way to give effect to the national policy expressed in Sec. 203(d) of the LMRA favoring final adjustment of disputes "by a method agreed upon by the parties," since no one would be allowed to determine what that method was in a particular case.

The principles of the *Trilogy* also seem to require that the arbitrator be free to resolve questions of substantive arbitrability. Arbitration is to be favored, said the Court, because the parties voluntarily select the arbitrator based on their "confidence in his knowledge of the common law of the shop" and their trust in his personal judg-

ment to bring to bear considerations not expressed in the contract. For these reasons the arbitrator is better qualified to decide contract interpretation questions than the "ablest judge."
Given the arbitrator's expertise, it would be contradictory to bind him by the superficial examination of a judge lacking that expertise.

In point of fact arbitrators can and do make
determinations of substantive arbitrability. The
vast majority of such determinations are made
in the first instance by the arbitrator and never
reviewed by the courts, but even when the courts
make the initial determination or have occasion to
review the arbitrator's ruling, the arbitrator's
decision usually governs. Some arbitrators explain their relationship to the courts on arbitrability questions by analogizing to the rules of evidence. A grievant may get to arbitration by presenting a *prima facie* case of arbitrability to a
court, but in order to prevail with the arbitrator
he must prove the issue arbitrable by the preponderance of his evidence on that question over
that of the other side.

Finally, even when an arbitrator is reluctant
to rule a grievance not arbitrable, he may achieve
the same result by ruling against the grievant on
the merits. By doing so he upholds the original
intentions of the parties without sacrificing the
therapeutic value of the arbitration process. The
therapy is not without cost, for it may defeat the

legitimate expectation of the parties that only certain matters would be arbitrable.

2. *Procedural Arbitrability*

In *John Wiley & Sons v. Livingston,* the Supreme Court held that questions of procedural arbitrability must be decided by the arbitrator rather than by the courts, for such matters are likely to be inextricably tied up with the merits of the case. The arbitrator's decisions on such questions will receive the same deference from the courts as his decisions on the merits of the dispute would receive. Thus courts have on numerous occasions rejected pleas that they review the decision of an arbitrator on timeliness, mootness, lack of specificity, and lack of a proper initiating party. *See, e. g., Carpenters Local No. 824, v. Brunswick Corp.,* 342 F.2d 792 (6th Cir. 1965).

Procedural arbitrability questions thus are more properly treated together with other decisions made by arbitrators, and the reader will find the subject discussed in more detail below.

B. ARBITRATORS AND THE LAW

Without question the most hotly debated issue within the arbitration community today is whether arbitrators may, should or must rule on questions of law that arise in connection with contractual grievances. There are three primary situations which force an arbitrator to grapple with this issue. In the first, the contract might appear to authorize or require some action arguably prohibited by law. One contract might specify the use of a seniority system challenged as being prohibited by civil rights laws. Another might call for wage increases in violation of wage and price controls (this was a frequent problem during the early 1970's when such controls were in effect). Still another might provide for piece rates that fall below the minimum wage established by the Fair Labor Standards Act.

In the second situation, the contract might prohibit certain conduct also arguably prohibited by law, and the arbitrator will be asked to apply (or not apply) the statutory standards to the contractual question. The most common cases are those in which the contract prohibits discrimination because of union activity, thus paralleling the National Labor Relations Act, or because of race, sex, religion or national origin, thus paralleling the civil rights laws.

A third situation is related to these two, but presents the issue from the other side. Certain conduct might be illegal only if it also violates the contract. A union might waive its statutory right to negotiate with the employer before the employer takes action on a mandatory subject of bargaining. The question then posed to the NLRB is whether it should defer to an arbitrator's decision (either before or after that opinion is rendered) on the contractual question in making its own decision on the unfair labor practice question. The next section treats the arbitrator's power to rule on legal questions. The two succeeding sections deal with the reactions of the Board and the courts to arbitration decisions involving such questions.

1.   The Authority of Arbitrators to Apply Federal or State Law

Most arbitrators would agree that in the second situation mentioned above, where contractual and legal provisions overlap but are not necessarily in conflict, an arbitrator could properly look at the positive law as an aid to interpreting the contract. Where the contract term is susceptible to two interpretations, one of which is consistent with the law and the other of which is in conflict with it, arbitrators may reasonably assume that the parties intended the lawful interpretation.

There is no agreement among arbitrators about their role in cases of a clear conflict between the law and the contract. The traditional position is that the arbitrator's sole function is to interpret the contract and that when such a conflict is present the arbitrator should respect the agreement and leave legal questions to the proper government officials. To do otherwise, the traditionalists hold, would be to exceed the scope of the submission agreement and the limits of any arbitral claim to expertise. Of course there is no problem if the parties ask the arbitrator for an opinion on the law, and if the parties incorporated legal standards in their agreement the arbitrator might be required to interpret the law.

The opposite position is taken by equally distinguished arbitrators, who point out that if the arbitrator ignores legal issues he may do the parties a disservice by requiring them to engage in further litigation. Some arbitrators believe that every collective bargaining agreement incorporates all applicable law—in other words, that the parties meant all of their agreement to be legal and desire the arbitrator to reform it to achieve that end if it is necessary to do so.

There are compromise positions to be found, too. Professor Archibald Cox, for one, has suggested that arbitrators should look to the law only to avoid rendering a decision that would **require** a party to break the law.

If the arbitrator does rule on a legal question in the course of interpreting a contract, should his interpretation be binding? Some have argued that because such issues are outside the arbitrator's authority and expertise, his ruling on the legal issue should be viewed as advisory only, subject to *de novo* review if the parties seek enforcement or vacation of the award in court. Professor Theodore St. Antoine of the University of Michigan has recently challenged this view. Arguing that the arbitrator is engaged as the parties' sole "contract reader," St. Antoine believes that if they intended him to answer legal issues in the course of that role his interpretation of the law should be binding **as between the parties.** If the arbitrator reads the Occupational Safety and Health Act in a proper case as imposing a stricter obligation on the employer than the reviewing court would find the law to require, the arbitrator's opinion should govern.

We are a long way from any final resolution of this dispute. For the moment it is sufficient to recognize the problem itself and the various positions arbitrators have taken.

2. The NLRB and the Arbitration Process

The attitudes of the NLRB toward the arbitration process and, more importantly, toward the relationship between that process and the unfair labor practice provisions of the LMRA have undergone several major changes in recent years. The problem of overlapping jurisdiction occurs chiefly in two types of cases, namely those where the legality of an act depends solely upon the interpretation of the collective bargaining agreement, and those where the contract is at most only one element bearing upon the legality of the act.

Representative of the first type is the "unilateral change" problem. Once a union is certified as the representative of a group of employees, the employer is obliged by Section 8(a)(5) of the Act to bargain with the union over "wages, hours and other terms and conditions of employment." By extension, this obligation applies to proposed changes in the terms of employment. One way an employer can fulfill this obligation is to bargain with the union for contractual authority to make certain changes during the term of the contract. If a dispute later arises over whether a particular change was authorized in the contract, resolution of the unfair labor practice charge may depend entirely on interpretation of the contract. Add a broad arbitration clause covering the issue and the result is a potential conflict of jurisdiction between the Board and the arbitrator.

The second type of case can be illustrated by a fairly common union security dispute. Section 8 (a)(3) prohibits discrimination against employees because of union membership or non-membership, except pursuant to a valid union security agreement. If an employer fires employee A for not joining the union, resolution of a Section 8(a)(3) charge might depend in part upon an interpretation of the contract (whether the union security clause applied to A and if so, whether he complied with it) and in part on the legal question whether the union security clause was actually valid under Section 8(a)(3). Here again there is a potential conflict of jurisdiction between the Board and an arbitrator.

In several cases in the 1960's the Supreme Court took the view that neither the Board nor the arbitrator was pre-empted in cases of overlapping jurisdiction. *Smith v. Evening News Ass'n,* 371 U.S. 195 (1962); *Carey v. Westinghouse Elec. Corp.,* 375 U.S. 261 (1964). It did say in the *Carey* case that if the two decision-makers disagreed the Board ruling would take precedence, but felt that the arbitration forum should be preserved because it might resolve the dispute or at least avoid fragmentation of the dispute because of the deference the Board showed toward arbitration awards.

That policy of deference to existing arbitration awards was stated most clearly in the Board's *Spielberg Mfg. Co.* decision, 112 N.L.R.B. 1080 (1955). There the Board agreed to accept the results of arbitration awards as conclusive on legal issues before the Board as a way of encouraging the voluntary settlement of labor disputes, provided that (1) the proceedings were fair and regular; (2) all parties had agreed to be bound by the award; and (3) the award was "not clearly repugnant to the purposes and policies" of the LMRA. In *Monsanto Chem. Co.,* 130 N.L.R.B. 1097 (1961), the Board added another requirement, that the arbitrator actually consider the issue that would be before the Board. When it attempted to back away from this requirement by introducing a principle of collateral estoppel (hold-

[*76*]

ing that the arbitration resolved issues which
could have been raised therein, regardless of
whether they were actually raised), it was quickly overruled by the Circuit Court of Appeals for
the District of Columbia, *Banyard v. NLRB,* 505
F.2d 342 (D.C.Cir. 1974).

The Board's deferral policy has been favorably
acknowledged by the Supreme Court both for representation issues (*Carey, supra*) and for unfair
labor practice issues, *NLRB v. C & C Plywood
Corp.,* 385 U.S. 421 (1967). In 1972 the Board
announced a major expansion of that policy. In
Collyer Insulated Wire, 192 N.L.R.B. 837 (1972)
it announced that it would defer to the arbitration
process **before** the arbitration decision is rendered
as well as after. That policy was consistently opposed by two members of the Board and in 1977
those dissenters won at least the partial support
of another member. In *General American Transportation Corp.,* 228 N.L.R.B. 808 (1977), a Section 8(a)(3) case, two members voted to defer to
arbitration, two voted not to defer, and in a separate opinion Member Murphy announced that in
her view the Board should only defer where the
dispute is essentially between the contracting parties and there is no claim of interference with individual employees' Section 7 rights. Accordingly she voted not to defer in that case but said that
she would defer in refusal to bargain cases, such
as the unilateral action example mentioned above.

A companion case, *Roy Robinson, Inc.,* 228 N.L.
R.B. 828 (1977), involved such a refusal to bargain. Member Murphy joined the two supporters
of the *Collyer* doctrine and by a 3–2 margin the
Board voted to defer to arbitration. Since those
decisions, one of the pro-deferral members has left
the Board and it is therefore likely that there will
be further developments in the Board's deferral
policy.

Member Murphy's concurrences in those cases
point out an important distinction: different types
of cases involve different criteria for decision, and
while arbitration may be the most appropriate
forum for some issues it may not be for all. Unilateral action cases are the most obvious choices
for deferral, for they frequently involve only a
contract interpretation question. Discriminatory
treatment cases may be less suitable for deferral
because the statutory rights of a third party, the
grieving employee, may be at stake. Representation and work-assignment disputes may well be the
least suited for arbitral resolution because the
Board applies different criteria to these cases than
those used by most arbitrators and because the arbitrator is unlikely to have all the competing parties (*i. e.,* the two or more unions claiming the
work or the representation rights) before him.

C. COURT DEFERRAL

1. *Labor Cases*

The *Steelworkers Trilogy* demonstrated that the courts will enforce arbitration agreements. Section 301 gives the courts jurisdiction to redress any breach of a collective bargaining agreement, however, which raises an interesting question: does the availability of arbitration mean that the courts may not or ought not deal with alleged contract breaches?

In *Drake Bakeries, Inc. v. Local 50, American Bakery Workers,* 370 U.S. 254 (1962), the employer brought a court action for damages caused by a strike in breach of contract. The federal district court ordered a stay in the action pending arbitration. On appeal to the Supreme Court, the employer argued that the parties could not have intended to arbitrate so fundamental a matter as a union strike in breach of the contract, and that in any event the strike amounted to a repudiation of the contract and thus freed the employer from any obligation to arbitrate. The Court rejected both claims. If breach of the no-strike clause was so fundamental, it held, the parties would have expressly excluded that issue from the arbitration provisions; and the company itself recognized the continued vitality of the contract by suing for damages pursuant to it and by continuing to apply its other provisions.

[*79*]

Drake Bakeries thus announced a policy of judicial deferral to arbitration, at least in cases where the issue would be the same in either forum. That decision depended upon the availability of arbitration to resolve the issue, however. Many contracts do not envision employer-filed grievances, though, and thus arbitration will not be available for resolution of claimed union breaches. In such a case court litigation may be the only remedy available to the employer, and the courts will not close their doors to the plaintiff. *Atkinson v. Sinclair Ref. Co.,* 370 U.S. 238 (1962). Arbitration is a voluntary process and will not be forced upon a party who has never agreed to be bound by it.

2. *Employment Discrimination Cases*

In employment discrimination cases the courts generally will not defer to arbitration, both because of a strong congressional desire to provide an additional remedy for employment discrimination and because certain distinctive aspects of arbitration make it a less appropriate forum for discrimination complaints than for other claims.

In *Alexander v. Gardner-Denver Co.,* 415 U.S. 36 (1974), the plaintiff argued before an arbitrator that his dismissal was in violation of the "just cause" and non-discrimination provisions of the collective bargaining agreement. The arbitrator made no reference in his opinion to the claim of racial discrimination but held that the petitioner had been discharged for just cause. Seven months later, the Equal Employment Opportunity Commission determined that there was not reasonable cause to believe that a violation of Title VII of the Civil Rights Act of 1964 had occurred and notified Alexander of his right to bring suit in the federal courts if he so desired. He did so, but the lower courts dismissed his action on the ground that, having chosen to arbitrate his grievance under the non-discrimination clause of the collective bargaining agreement, he was bound by the adverse result and thereby precluded from suing his employer under Title VII.

The Supreme Court unanimously reversed and held that Alexander's Title VII right to a trial was not foreclosed by the adverse arbitration award. The Court first noted that Congress had clearly intended Title VII rights to supplement other remedies, not replace them. It analogized the situation to the overlap between arbitration and the LMRA found in *Carey v. Westinghouse Elec. Corp.*, 375 U.S. 261 (1964). As in that case, the procedures in discrimination cases were said to be complementary rather than exclusive since "consideration of the claim by both forums may promote the policies underlying each."

The Court then rejected the argument that contractual provision and actual use of the arbitration procedure constituted a waiver of Title VII rights. There can be no prospective waiver by the union of an individual's Title VII rights, it said, and "mere resort" by the individual to the arbitration procedure constitutes no such waiver. The Court did admit that an individual might make a "voluntary and knowing" express waiver as part of a formal settlement to a Title VII cause of action, but Alexander had not done so. The Court also stated that the preclusion argument advanced by the Company would not be proper in light of the different functions of arbitrator and judge. The arbitrator sits to apply the contract; he has no independent general authority to invoke public laws.

The Court even declined to adopt a policy of deferral to arbitration awards for the same reason it rejected the preclusion argument. The arbitrator's role is to effectuate the parties' intent, not the purposes of the Civil Rights law. In addition, the specialized competence of arbitrators is in the law of the shop, not the law of the land, and the factfinding process of arbitration is not equivalent to judicial factfinding. If the courts were to impose a strict deferral standard, they would tend to make arbitration more complex, expensive and time-consuming, and thus detract from its greatest advantages.

The Court did not completely foreclose arbitration of discrimination cases. The arbitration decision could be admitted as evidence in the trial and be "accorded such weight as the court deems appropriate." In a (relatively) famous footnote to that statement, the Court gave some indication of what it had in mind:

> 21. We adopt no standards as to the weight to be accorded an arbitral decision, since this must be determined in the court's discretion with regard to the facts and circumstances of each case. Relevant factors include the existence of provisions in the collective-bargaining agreement that conform substantially with Title VII, the degree of procedural fairness in the arbitral forum, adequacy of the record with respect to the issue of discrimination, and the special competence of particular arbitrators. Where an arbitral determination gives full consideration to an employee's Title VII rights, a court may properly accord it great weight. This is especially true where the issue is solely one of fact, specifically addressed by the parties and decided by the arbitrator on the basis of an adequate record. But courts should ever be mindful that Congress, in enacting Title VII, thought it necessary to provide a judicial forum for the ultimate resolution of discriminatory employment claims. It is the duty of courts to assure the full availability of this forum.

That statement seems to indicate that arbitration could yet play an important role in the resolution of discrimination cases, but to date that has not happened.

Parties to collective bargaining agreements have been noticeably cautious in amending arbitration provisions to comply with the standards of footnote 21, perhaps because they realize, as the Court did, that arbitration under such conditions would be nearly as formal, expensive and slow as a court suit. In the few recorded cases where parties have consciously tried to comply with those standards the cases never reached federal court—some involved the "voluntary and knowing" waiver that would preclude court action, and most resulted in awards favorable to the grievant, which would obviate a Title VII suit. In a few other cases federal courts have given arbitral awards some weight as evidence. The American Arbitration Association has established an arbitration procedure modelled after the footnote 21 requirements, and it is therefore possible that a modified form of arbitration will come to be used in these cases.

D. JUDICIAL REVIEW OF ARBITRATION AWARDS

Arbitration awards come before the courts in one of three ways: either the prevailing party seeks judicial enforcement of the award against a loser who refuses to comply with it, or the losing party seeks to have the award set aside because of some alleged substantive or procedural error, or one of the parties (or a third party, such as an individual employee covered by collective bargaining agreement) invokes an arbitration award to buttress its case in a collateral judicial proceeding.

The basic rules governing judicial review of arbitration awards were announced by the Supreme Court in the last of the *Steelworkers Trilogy* cases, *United Steelworkers of America v. Enterprise Wheel & Car Corp.,* 363 U.S. 593 (1960). An arbitrator in that case had ordered reinstatement with back pay, after the expiration of the collective bargaining agreement, of certain employees discharged during the term of the agreement. The Court of Appeals refused to order the reluctant employer to comply with the arbitration award because of the failure of the award to specify the exact amount due the employees, because back pay could not be awarded for any time after expiration of the contract, and because the order of reinstatement was unenforceable due to the expiration of the agreement.

The Supreme Court reversed. Mr. Justice Douglas wrote the opinion of the Court but spoke only for four members because three concurred separately, one took no part, and one dissented. "The refusal of courts to review the merits of an arbitration award is the proper approach to arbitration under collective bargaining agreements," said Justice Douglas. "The federal policy of settling labor disputes by arbitration would be undermined if courts had the final say on the merits of the awards."

To be sure, the arbitrator's power is not unlimited. He is "confined to interpretation and application of the collective bargaining agreement; he does not sit to dispense his own brand of industrial justice," and his award is legitimate "only so long as it draws its essence from the collective bargaining agreement. When the arbitrator's words manifest an infidelity to this obligation, courts have no choice but to refuse enforcement of the award."

These exceptions are not to be taken too liberally. The "essence" of the award must be drawn from the agreement, but the arbitrator may "look for guidance from many sources" including, presumably, those cited in *Warrior & Gulf*: the practices of the industry and the shop, "the effect upon productivity of a particular result, its consequence to the morale of the shop, his judgment whether tensions will be heightened or diminished." And if this does not give the arbitrator enough leeway, the courts are further restricted in their review for "a mere ambiguity in the opinion accompanying an award, which permits the inference that the arbitrator may have exceeded his authority, is not a reason for refusing to enforce the award."

In the *Enterprise Wheel* case itself, the arbitrator's opinion was ambiguous and may have been based solely upon the arbitrator's view of the requirements of enacted legislation rather than on the contract. It was not clear that he exceeded the scope of the submission, however, and according to Justice Douglas the Court of Appeals was therefore wrong to replace his construction of the contract with its own.

It should not be surprising that courts have been hesitant to overrule arbitrators since the *Enterprise Wheel* decision. Indeed, relatively few arbitration awards are ever challenged in court because the futility of doing so is apparent in most cases. Nevertheless, not all courts have been willing to abdicate their authority, and it is not by any means certain that they should do so. The United States Arbitration Act, one of the sources of the federal common law of labor arbitration created by the courts since the *Lincoln Mills* decision, specifically authorizes vacation of arbitration awards on a number of grounds (Appendix 6, Section 10), as does the proposed Uniform Arbitration Act (Appendix 7, Section 12).

There have been several successful challenges to arbitration awards in the years since the *Enterprise Wheel* decision. These can be classified under five headings: (1) Lack of jurisdiction or authority for the award; (2) Procedural unfairness or irregularity; (3) Gross error or irrationality; (4) Violation of law or public policy; and (5) Ambiguity, incompleteness or inconsistency.

1. Lack of Jurisdiction or Authority for the Award

By far the most common reason for setting aside an arbitrator's award is that the arbitrator was not authorized to make the award. This situation can come about in a number of ways. The most obvious case occurs when the arbitrator ignores, in the words of the *Warrior & Gulf* decision, an "express provision excluding a particular grievance from arbitration" or "the most forceful evidence of a purpose to exclude the claim from arbitration." This is, of course, the old question of "substantive arbitrability." Thus an arbitration clause covering a certain contract "and amendments thereto" will not allow an award based on wage rates contained in a subsequent agreement that was not an amendment of the initial contract. *IBEW Local 278 v. Jetero Corp.*, 496 F.2d 661 (5th Cir. 1974). Of course if the parties agree to let the arbitrator himself decide the substantive arbitrability issue, his decision will be subject only to the same limited review appropriate for an arbitrator's award on the merits.

There are less obvious ways in which an arbitrator's substantive authority may be limited. One is by the absence of a valid, binding agreement. If the alleged agreement had expired, had been obtained by fraud, or was not properly ratified, a court may hold that an arbitrator lacked authority to apply the terms of the document—or indeed, that there could be no arbitration at all if the arbitration agreement itself was contained only in the challenged document.   Another restriction comes from the submission agreement, for the parties can submit an issue to the arbitrator that is narrower than the arbitration clause itself might allow.   For example, a standard arbitration clause might provide for arbitration of any dispute over the "meaning, interpretation or application of this agreement" but the parties might ask the arbitrator simply to determine a factual issue, say whether or not Employee X lied on his application form. If so, the arbitrator has authority only to deal with the submission and any rulings on other questions could properly be set aside by a court.   *Cf. Textile Workers Union of America Local 1386 v. American Thread Co.,* 291 F.2d 894 (4th Cir. 1961).

An arbitrator's authority to issue a particular remedy may also be limited by the parties.   Arbitrators frequently hold that although an employee engaged in some misconduct, the punishment levied by the employer was too severe and must be reduced.   To prevent such second guessing, employers often bargain for and sometimes obtain contract clauses prohibiting arbitral modification of discipline.   An arbitrator's award disregarding such a remedial limitation would properly be set aside, *e. g. Amanda Bent Bolt Co. v. UAW Local 1549,* 451 F.2d 1277 (6th Cir. 1971).

At least in theory, an arbitrator would be similarly bound to respect procedural limitations expressed in the collective bargaining agreement and could be reversed if he did not do so. As noted above, however, the courts regard these questions as peculiarly suited for an arbitrator's determination and will not readily overturn such a determination once it is rendered. Still, if a contract prohibits arbitration unless the union has demanded it within a certain period, the arbitrator would exceed his authority if he ignored that limitation absent waiver, estoppel or the like. In practice most arbitrators either respect such limitations or have strong enough reasons for not applying them that courts seldom reverse them.

Finally there is a broad category of arbitral error that is open to judicial abuse. Many contracts provide that an arbitrator may not "alter, modify or add to" the contract and every award must at least "draw its essence" from the collective bargaining agreement. This is not entirely consistent with the recognized power of the arbitrator to look beyond the four corners of the agreement to determine what the contract means. Negotiating history may cast light on the meaning of an ambiguous clause, and a consistent practice of long duration might be regarded as a tacit amendment of the contract—but at the same time an arbitrator's decision premised on such evidence would look suspiciously like a modification of or an addition to the contract.

The most famous instance of a court applying this approach in reviewing an arbitrator's award is *Torrington Co. v. Metal Products Workers Local 1645,* 362 F.2d 677 (2d Cir. 1966), a decision that has been roundly criticized by almost every arbitrator who has had the opportunity to comment on it. For many years the employer had paid employees for one hour away from work on Election Day, but this practice had not been incorporated in the contract. Prior to contract negotiations one year the employer announced that it would no longer pay for that hour. The contract ultimately signed was as silent on the point as its predecessors. When the employer refused to pay for the accustomed hour, the union took the case to arbitration and secured an award that the Election Day pay could be terminated only by mutual agreement. The federal district and appeals courts denied enforcement of the award, holding that it constituted an addition to or modification of the contract and was thus outside the arbitrator's authority. Critical commentators have pointed out that the courts were substituting their judgment on the merits for that of the arbitrator, for his decision simply held that the past practice was, in fact, part of the contract; the parties, in other words, had amended the written agreement by their actions and the arbitrator merely gave force to that amendment.

A similar decision is that in *H. K. Porter Co. v. United Saw, File & Steel Products Workers,* 333 F. 2d 596 (3d Cir. 1964). The contract in that case expressly limited eligibility for pensions to those employees 65 years old who had at least 25 years of service. Without the support of past practice, the arbitrator held that employees over 65 with less than 25 years of service were entitled to a prorated pension when they were terminated as a result of a plant removal. The court held that the arbitrator had tried to administer "his own brand of industrial justice" and proceeded to revise his award to reflect the court's view of the parties' intentions.

Although both *Torrington* and *H. K. Porter Co.* talk of the arbitrator's lack of authority for his award, both involved a review of the merits of the cases and a substitution of the court's view of the merits for that of the arbitrator. Both cases seem to be exceptions, however. Few courts are likely to intrude as deeply into arbitral prerogatives.

2. *Procedural Unfairness or Irregularity*

A procedural defect which makes an arbitration fundamentally unfair would be very likely to cause a reviewing court to set aside the resulting award.

The clearest cases are also among the rarest: bribery, corruption or fraud will certainly deprive the award of the general respect owing to arbitrator's decisions, but such cases are few and far between. Bias on the part of the arbitrator will also cause the award to be set aside. Such bias can be inferred from an undisclosed close affiliation with one of the parties or from evident partiality in the conduct of the hearing.

Even less frequently will an evidentiary ruling cause an award to be set aside. The rules of evidence normally do not bind an arbitrator and rulings on such questions are seldom challenged, but a severely prejudicial admission or exclusion of evidence can taint the proceedings. In one such case, where evidentiary technicalities had not been applied in the past, an arbitrator refused to allow introduction of certain evidence in rebuttal on the ground that it should have been presented as part of the case in chief; the district court vacated the award, stating that the application without warning of such a strict rule denied a fair hearing. *Harvey Aluminum Inc. v. United Steelworkers of America, AFL–CIO,* 263 F.Supp. 488 (C.D.Cal. 1967). In an earlier case an award was vacated in part because the arbitrator relied on a previous arbitral award referred to in the hearing but never actually introduced. *Textile Workers Union of America Local 1386 v. American Thread Co.,* 291 F.2d 894 (4th Cir. 1961). Other errors that might provide grounds for judicial review would include denial of opportunity for cross-examination or refusal of a reasonable request for a continuance.

Finally, there seems to be little reason to believe that breaches of procedural requirements established by state laws will cause a court to set aside an arbitrator's ruling, at least where those requirements interfere with the federal policy favoring the arbitration process. *West Rock Lodge No. 2120, I.A.M. v. Geometric Tool Co.,* 406 F.2d 284 (2d Cir. 1968).

3. *Gross Error or Irrationality*

The Supreme Court plainly did not want judges reviewing arbitrators' decisions on the merits, but some lower courts have read into the *Enterprise Wheel* opinion an implied exception for cases of gross error. A judicial finding that an arbitrator with proper jurisdiction who conducted a fair hearing nevertheless reached the wrong result seems to be just what the Supreme Court tried to prevent, however, and courts engaging in such a review process have used a variety of terms to distinguish their cases from *Enterprise Wheel.* A few cases have relied on an admittedly erroneous assumption of fact by the arbitrator. Others have introduced a minimum standard of rationality, sometimes stated in terms of a decision that an "honest intellect" or some "judge, or group of judges" could conceivably reach, and sometimes stated negatively, as prohibiting a "capricious, unreasonable interpretation" and an award that is "wholly baseless and completely without reason."

Such strenuous language does not entirely hide the fact that the courts involved are still reviewing the merits of the arbitrator's decision. Indeed, it is reasonable to assume that in bargaining for arbitration the parties assumed that the arbitrator would be reasonable; setting aside an irrational decision would thus be entirely consistent with their intentions. The difficulty of course comes in separating decisions that are only arguably wrong from those that are completely irrational. That difficulty is compounded by the fact in almost every case one of the two parties argued for just such an award, and would not be likely to view it as irrational.

4. *Violation of Law or Public Policy*

The split in the arbitration community over the role of the arbitrator in cases of conflict between the contract and the law has already been discussed. Many believe that the arbitrator should enforce the contract and ignore the law, and almost as many hold the opposite.

Whichever approach the arbitrator adopts, the function of the courts is clear: they will not enforce an arbitration order sustaining or commanding illegal conduct. As one court put it,

> [I]t is too plain for argument that no court will order a party to do something, if in order

to comply with the court's directive, he must commit a crime. This is so despite any protestations that the party contracted to do what it is said that he should be ordered to do.

UAW Local 985 v. W. M. Chace Co., 262 F.Supp. 114 (E.D.Mich.1966). This attitude involves no conflict with the *Enterprise Wheel* strictures on judicial review, for it involves only a determination of the lawfulness of enforcing an award, not a review of the correctness of the arbitrator's interpretation of the contract.

There are many laws which could be violated by conduct required by a collective bargaining agreement. The most common case involves alleged unfair labor practices. This raises a complicating factor, for the NLRB has exclusive jurisdiction over unfair labor practices. Where the NLRB has already spoken, the court will simply adopt its view of the legality of the conduct required by the arbitration award. Where the Board has not yet ruled, the courts have themselves made the determination of legality. This is not as surprising as it might seem, for the district courts are charged in other contexts, in Sections 10(j) and 10(*l*) injunction proceedings for example, with making preliminary determinations on alleged unfair labor practices, and their decisions are subject to review in the same courts of appeal that review NLRB decisions.

Courts have been just as reluctant to require conduct in violation of antitrust and anti-kickback legislation. Following *Alexander v. Gardner-Denver Co.*, it is beyond question that a court would not enforce an arbitration award requiring discriminatory treatment, a situation that occasionally arises when an employer unilaterally changes terms or conditions of employment to avoid a charge of race or sex discrimination and the union obtains an award prohibiting the change. The situation is less clear when the discriminatory treatment is in fact reverse discrimination taken pursuant to settlement agreement with an anti-discrimination agency. Most arbitrators would not disturb the employer's action on contractual grounds in such a case, and it is not at all clear what a reviewing court would do if an arbitrator did so.

There have been some suggestions, but few direct holdings, that courts could deny enforcement of an award that is inconsistent with some strong public policy, even if the conduct required by the award is not prohibited by law. In the case most frequently cited (and criticized) in this connection, the California Supreme Court vacated an arbitrator's order to reinstate a discharged Communist, even though the arbitrator found that the real reason for the discharge was union activity, not Communism. *Black v. Cutter Laboratories*, 43 Cal.2d 788, 278 P.2d 905 (1955), cert.

dismissed 351 U.S. 292 (1955), reh. denied 352 U.S. 859 (1956). The court cited federal and state laws banning Communist Party activity and held that those laws established a public policy sufficiently strong to void an arbitration order of reinstatement to work "in a plant which produces antibiotics used by both the military and civilians." Later cases on other issues have affirmed the public policy principle but have interpreted it narrowly.

5. Incompleteness, Ambiguity or Inconsistency

The last of the most common grounds for judicial review is of a different nature, and involves defects in the arbitration award itself. If the award is incomplete, by not answering the issue posed for example, a court may be unable to enforce it as it stands. Given the alternatives of amending the award or resubmitting it to the arbitrator, most courts would deny enforcement and follow the latter option. Similarly, if the award is so ambiguous as to defy understanding, the appropriate action for the court to take would be resubmission to the arbitrator for clarification.

Finally, an award that is internally inconsistent may not be in suitable shape for judicial enforcement, but inconsistency with a prior award in the same plant will not bar enforcement. Different readings of the same contract or conflicting actions required by different contracts can best be resolved by negotiation. This may leave one party in an awkward, expensive position, but the courts deem that preferable to judicial intervention in the dispute resolution procedure chosen by that party.

6. *Individual Challenges: The Duty of Fair Representation*

Each of the previously discussed grounds for judicial review of arbitration awards presumes that a party to the collective bargaining agreement is attacking the award. The only way individual employees, who are not parties to the contract, can challenge an award is by first proving that the arbitration was tainted by the failure of the union to represent them fairly—proving, in other words, that the union breached the duty of fair representation recognized in a long series of cases beginning with *Steele v. Louisville & Nashville Railroad,* 323 U.S. 192 (1944). Once that hurdle is cleared, the employees must then prove that the employer did in fact break the contract.

Cases in 1962 and 1965 held that employees could maintain a Section 301 action against employer breaches of contract provided they first attempted to exhaust contractual grievance and arbitration procedures. In *Vaca v. Sipes,* 386 U.S. 171 (1967), the Supreme Court allowed an employee to sue his union in a Section 301 action for breach of the duty of fair representation in its

[*99*]

handling of a grievance. The employer in that case refused to reinstate one Owens for health reasons after he was hospitalized for heart disease. The union processed his grievance through the contractual steps but after receiving a negative report from a doctor selected by Owens himself the union declined to take the case to arbitration. The Supreme Court recognized that in some instances aggrieved employees were entitled to court review of a union's processing of a grievance, but stated that allowing every individual to force arbitration would undermine the collective bargaining relationship and overburden the arbitration process. Such an action under Section 301 should be allowed, the Court said, only when the union's conduct was "arbitrary, discriminatory or in bad faith." If the grievant can prove the breach of the duty of fair representation he would be entitled to sue the employer directly even if the contract included a mandatory arbitration clause. In the event the grievant prevailed over both the union and the employer, the union would be liable for any increase in the damages suffered by the employee as a result of its wrongful conduct, and the employer would be liable for the remainder.

That much is simply background for the current topic. If the union does in fact take the case to arbitration but breaches its duty of fair representation in handling the case it is liable for damages, but can the "tainted" arbitration award stand? Can an employer who breached the contract in good faith stand behind such an award and claim the benefit of the finality established by *Enterprise Wheel?*

In *Hines v. Anchor Motor Freight Inc.,* 424 U.S. 554 (1976), the Court answered both of these questions in the negative. There a joint area committee (JAC) composed of equal numbers of employer and union representatives upheld the discharge of several employees for falsification of expense vouchers. The employees filed a Section 301 action claiming that the union had breached its duty of fair representation by not properly investigating the case and that the employer had breached the contract because the employees were not guilty of the offense charged.

The lower courts dismissed the action against the employer because the JAC decision was final and binding. Questionably treating the JAC as the equivalent of an arbitration board, the Supreme Court reversed, holding that a union's breach of the duty of fair representation

> relieves the employee of an express or implied requirement that disputes be settled through contractual procedures and, if it seriously undermines the integrity of the arbitral process, also removes the bar of the finality provision of the contract.

[*101*]

In other words, a "tainted" process does not protect the employer who wrongfully but in good faith breaches the contract.

Although the question of what constitutes a union breach of the duty of fair representation was not at issue before the Court, it offered several comments on that subject, suggesting that the union's decisions must be made "honestly and in good faith and without invidious discrimination or arbitrary conduct," and cannot be "dishonest, in bad faith or discriminatory."

By any standard the *Hines* decision seriously breached the finality attributed to arbitration awards after *Enterprise Wheel*. Just how serious that breach is, or in simpler terms, just how easy it will be for individual employees to overturn arbitration awards, will depend on the breadth the courts give to such terms as "arbitrary" and "bad faith." Most of the cases decided in the lower courts after *Vaca* have had a showing of malice or hostility, but a number of cases have gone further. In *Holodnak v. Avco Corp.*, 381 F. Supp. 191 (D.Conn.1974), aff'd in relevant part, 514 F.2d 285 (2d Cir.), cert. denied 423 U.S. 892 (1975), the district court vacated the award and faulted the union attorney for overlooking some legal arguments and for not being sufficiently aggressive in protecting the grievant's rights. Other courts have gone so far as to equate negligence in handling a case with the arbitrary conduct mentioned in *Vaca v. Sipes*.

There will surely be much more litigation on this point, but at the moment it is clear that *Enterprise Wheel* does not present an insurmountable barrier to an attack by individual employees on an arbitration award, provided that the employees can show that the award was tainted by union malfeasance or nonfeasance.

V

LEGAL ASPECTS OF THE ARBI-
TRATION PROCESS

The previous section dealt with the relationship between arbitration and other dispute-resolution forums. This section concerns only the legal aspects of the arbitration process itself. Even the term "legal aspects" might be overstated, for many of the issues discussed herein are really matters of custom rather than law, even though the courts might in some cases adopt those customs as law. The title of the section is appropriate, nevertheless, if it is read as referring to the "common law of arbitration," much as the Supreme Court in the *Steelworkers Trilogy* spoke of "the common law of the shop." Mention will be made of court rulings where appropriate, but the main objective of the section is to explore how arbitrators treat these problems of interpretation and procedure.

A. THE ARBITRATION CLAUSE AND ITS MEANING: ARBITRABILITY FROM THE ARBITRATOR'S POINT OF VIEW

1. *Substantive Arbitrability*

The so-called "standard" arbitration clause reads as follows:

> Any unresolved dispute involving the interpretation or application of any provision of this agreement shall be submitted to arbitration. The arbitrator shall have no authority to add to, subtract from, or modify the provisions of this agreement.

For simplicity's sake, the following discussion of substantive arbitrability assumes the existence of such a standard clause, and the absence of any specific inclusions or exclusions. The reader should keep in mind that variations in language, particularly toward the "broad" or "all-disputes" type of arbitration clause will very likely produce quite different results. The standard clause has been chosen for discussion because it is the more common of the two general types and because arbitrability questions are more likely to arise in connection with its narrower language.

As noted above, the courts have consistently held that questions of substantive arbitrability are for the courts to determine, even if their only function is the superficial investigation of whether a particular dispute is "on its face" subject to the arbitration clause. If that were all there was to arbitrability questions, there would be no need for this section. As also noted above, though, arbitrators do in fact decide substantive arbitrability issues. Some contracts specify that such preliminary questions are for the arbitrator. Others do not so specify but in practice the parties raise these questions in arbitration rather than litigation. And in still other cases, arbitrators are asked to make a *de novo* determination on substantive arbitrability after a court has determined that the contract "on its face" provides for arbitration of the dispute. Thus it becomes important to know how arbitrators react to claims that a particular issue is not arbitrable. For purposes of discussion, the realm of labor relations issues arguably subject to arbitration can be divided into three categories: (a) Issues involving the type and number of jobs and employees covered by the agreement; (b) Issues involving the level or amount of contract wages or benefits; and (c) Issues involving the range of subjects with which the agreement concerns itself. The following discussion relies heavily on Frank Plaut's thorough treatment of this subject, "Arbitrability Under the Standard Labor Arbitration Clause," 14 *Arbitration Journal* 51 (1959).

(a) *Issues Involving the Type and Number of Jobs and Employees Covered by the Agreement.* This category includes the most fundamental aspect of the employment relationships, the connection between work and workers. Subjects falling within this category are generally held to be arbitrable, for the whole agreement would be illusory if workers could be separated from their work without a strong justification.

Subcontracting, for example, could eliminate the bargaining unit if carried to an extreme. On the other hand, it might involve no measurable loss to the bargaining unit, as when it is *de minimis* or concerns only work the bargaining unit employees are not capable of doing. In the absence of a contractual restriction on subcontracting the union must show at least that subcontracting impairs substantial rights established elsewhere in the agreement. (In order to prevail on the merits, it may also be necessary to show that the challenged actions were taken chiefly to avoid those other obligations.) The obvious example would be the total subcontracting of all bargaining unit work to a non-union plant. Less obvious, but still arbitrable cases would include subcontracting simply to avoid paying contractual wages or overtime, or to escape union work rules. By contrast, subcontracting of major construction work never previously performed by bargaining unit members would not impair the wages or benefits clauses of the collective bargaining agreement and would not be arbitrable in the absence of a specific requirement to that effect.

The standard arbitration clause will usually be held to cover disputes over whether certain employees are within or without the bargaining unit and disputes over whether certain jobs constitute bargaining unit work. Both of these types of cases will involve interpretation of the recognition clause, and it would be hard to argue in most cases that the meaning of the recognition clause was so clear that such grievances could not possibly have merit.

Termination disputes present the most difficult cases in this category. The vast majority of collective bargaining agreements contain some limitation on discharges, usually of the "just cause" variety. If a contract does **not** contain such a clause, is the employer free to discharge at will? As with the subcontracting cases, allegations of employer intent to evade other contract provisions, *e. g.* seniority, vacation pay, or pension obligations, will raise arbitrable issues, but in the absence of such allegations arbitrators differ on arbitrability. Some take the view that termination is so fundamental an issue that limitations on management action in this regard are implied in **all** collective bargaining agreements. That assumption is a two-edged sword, however: if it is such a fundamental issue, contractual silence must have been intentional and the arbitrator has no business adding limitations on employer action to the contract.

(b) *Issues Involving the Level or Amount of Contract Wages or Benefits.* This category can be further divided into two types of cases calling for different presumptions about arbitrability. Grievances demanding a change in the general structure of wages or benefits, or in the standards used to determine them, are generally not arbitrable. Such matters are almost always set by negotiation and cannot be resolved by interpretation of the existing agreement. Arbitrators possess no authority to rewrite the terms of a contract, and will usually refuse even to hear a claim that they ought to do so. This may not always be so with regard to wage-reopener provisions. In a few cases where the parties have been unable to agree on a new wage scale after negotiations pursuant to such a clause arbitrators have heard and resolved the subsequent grievance. Even this very limited occurrence probably represents a minority view.

The second type of case is quite different. Where the question is the application of a wage structure to individual cases rather than the setting of that structure, most arbitrators will take jurisdiction. Looked at differently, this type of dispute is a standard, garden-variety interpretation question and there is no reason to deny arbitrability.

(c) *Issues Involving the Range of Subjects with Which the Contract Concerns Itself.* Falling within this category are matters that are normally the subject of negotiation such as hours, job descriptions, and seniority. As a general rule the existence of such rights is not arbitrable, but once established by negotiation the application of those rights is subject to arbitration.

For example, an arbitrator is unlikely to rule on the merits of a union claim that he should create seniority rights where none existed previously or that he should extend existing seniority rights to cover new types of decisions. If the grievance alleges that an individual's seniority has been improperly calculated or that the employer did not follow negotiated seniority rules, however, the dispute will almost certainly be held arbitrable.

The same principle applies in another area. Absent some contractual limitation, complaints about changes in the **job process**, such as introduction or discontinuance of product lines or mechanization of a job formerly done by hand, will not be arbitrable. A simple change in the speed at which some task is to be performed or the addition of duties to an existing job may well be arbitrable, however.

Similarly, most arbitrators would not take jurisdiction over a grievance seeking to create through arbitration a new benefit such as severance pay, but most would find arbitrable a claim that some existing benefit such as vacation pay has "vested" and must be paid if an employee is discharged.

(d) *Summary*. At some risk of over-generalization these rules can be simply summarized: arbitrators will usually find arbitrable grievances involving. (i) the interpretation or application of terms included in the collective bargaining agreement; (ii) alleged violations of a definite and clear past practice; and, less certainly, (iii) items which, if held not to be arbitrable, might impair or negate a substantial right established in the agreement. Arbitrators will generally hold not arbitrable (i) disputes over subjects not covered in the collective bargaining agreement or in a definite and clear past practice, if silence on the point seems to be deliberate; and (ii) complaints over impasses in areas subject to negotiation.

2. *Procedural Arbitrability*

There is an almost infinite variety of procedural defects that can be cited as reasons for preventing arbitration, but discussion of two of the most common should illustrate the reaction of arbitrators to such claims.

(a) *Time Limitations.* Many contracts establish rigid limits on the time in which a grievance can be filed, on the processing of the grievance through the grievance procedure, and on the demand for and completion of arbitration. Other contracts have less rigid provisions and it is at least arguable that a rule of reasonableness, akin to the equitable doctrine of laches, is implied in all agreements.

Where the time limitations are clear, a breach of them will usually be held by an arbitrator to make the case non-arbitrable, however strong the case might be on the merits. In part this simply represents the will of the parties who must have meant "ten days" if they said "ten days." In part, it also represents a recognition that an effective grievance procedure requires quick and efficient processing of grievances. If the arbitrator waives adherence to agreed rules, he contributes at the same time to a weakening of the process which those rules were created to protect.

But "the law abhors forfeitures", and so do arbitrators. As a result, they will eagerly look for reasons why a case is arbitrable even though the grievance has been filed or processed late. One obvious case where that should be is fraud, as when a party deliberately gets the other to delay action until the time limitation passes and then refuses to proceed because of the violation. A less reprehensible situation occurs where such a delay has been requested for the requestor's convenience. In such an event the arbitrator is likely to hold that the requestor is estopped from asserting the time limitation. A third exception involves explicit or implied waivers, as when the parties have ignored the time limitations in the past without forfeiture of arbitration rights or when settlement efforts continue beyond the time period specified for some further action. A fourth category involves "continuing injuries", such as the refusal of an employer to pay a worker the wage established for the classification to which he is assigned. In such cases the arbitrator may hold that the time limit for filing grievances recommences each day. (This cannot be asserted to justify repetitious grievances, where an earlier one on the same issue was resolved against the grievant.) Finally, an arbitrator may compromise the issue, holding that breach of the time limitation does not prevent arbitration but does limit the remedy available.

(b) *Changed Issues.* Suppose a union files a grievance alleging that the employer improperly assigned work to non-unit personnel, but at the arbitration hearing argues instead that those persons are actually members of the unit who deserve the higher pay the contract provides. May the arbitrator decide the new issue? Most arbitrators would not do so, absent a stipulation by both parties. Normally the arbitrator will decide only those issues raised in the grievance process. To do otherwise would allow unfair advantage to be taken of the surprised party. That would weaken the grievance procedure itself, and that in turn would mean that in the future matters that could be settled between parties might be withheld until the arbitration hearing. While this does not mean that the grievance form filled out on the shop floor must read like a legal pleading, it does mean each party is entitled to know prior to the arbitration hearing the essential claims and evidence on which the other relies.

B. SOME PROBLEMS OF DUE PROCESS AND INDIVIDUAL RIGHTS

There have been a number of suggestions in the scholarly literature on labor arbitration that both substantive and procedural constitutional rights ought to be recognized by arbitrators. Public employers and perhaps some private employers so closely regulated by a government agency as to function as an arm of that agency may well be subject to the Constitution. Because the Constitution only restricts the powers of governments, however, most employers are not so directly constrained, and arbitrators have been reluctant to add a wide range of limitations on management action in the guise of contractual interpretation.

Still, constitutional protections have had an undeniable impact on labor arbitration. Arbitrators occasionally refer to constitutional cases in determining whether certain employee actions constitute just cause for discharge, and they quite frequently are influenced by constitutional notions of "due process" in the course of their own rulings on procedural questions. Courts are even more likely to insist on compliance with constitutional requirements before committing judicial power to the enforcement of an arbitration award.

The purpose of this section is to explore the treatment by arbitrators and courts of certain issues arising in arbitration that correspond to problems of criminal procedure. One of the primary areas of this overlap between private and public procedure, the duty of fair representation, has already been discussed, but there are many other areas where such questions are likely to arise. The following pages deal with the most important of these.

1. Notice

The relationship between the individual employee and the arbitration process is marked by some confusion. Traditionally arbitrators and the courts have held that the employer and the union were the only parties to a collective bargaining agreement and that the individual employee had no role in arbitration and no rights except as his representative, the union, chose to assert them. (Of course the agreement could create a role or enforceable rights, and the employee has long been able to demand that the union fairly represent him in all its actions.) This traditional approach has been modified somewhat in recent years. The NLRB has indicated that it will not defer to an arbitration award where an individual employee's interests do not coincide with those of his union unless the employee is given notice of the time and place of the arbitration hearing, or unless it can be shown that his interests were fully represented by one of the parties. One federal district court incorporated a notice requirement in the duty of fair representation where the grievant was the only affected employee, *Thompson v. IAM Lodge 1049,* 258 F.Supp. 235 (E.D.Va. 1966), but the attempt of a state court to require notification of an entire group of employees whose rights could be affected by the seniority grievance at issue, *Clark v. Hein-Werner Corp.,* 8 Wis.2d 264, 99 N.W.2d 132 (1959), cert. denied 362 U.S. 962 (1960), has been widely criticized among arbitrators. The principle enunciated in support of the Wisconsin court's decision, that

> where the interests of two groups of employees are diametrically opposed to each other and the union espouses the cause of one in the arbitration, it follows as a matter of law that there has been no fair representation of the other group. This is true even though . . . the union acts completely objectively and with the best of motives.

has been rejected by the Supreme Court. In *Humphrey v. Moore,* 375 U.S. 335 (1964), the Court found no violation in a union action that favored one group of employees over another, for the union acted in good faith upon relevant considerations.

Arbitrators in serious disciplinary cases generally require that the employee be notified of the actual charges against him and will usually not permit discipline to be later defended on the basis of other charges. They are unlikely to require formal notice of the arbitration hearing so long as the union is present to defend the grievant's position.

2. *Separate Representation and Intervention*

The union's representation of the employee will in most cases fulfill the right to counsel and obviate the need for any form of employee intervention. Indeed, most unions strenuously resist any direct intervention by separate counsel for the employee because of a belief that it would undercut the union's role as exclusive representative of the entire bargaining unit. Arbitrators have been reluctant to permit formal employee intervention, again because of the position that arbitration is the creature of the parties, the employer and the union, to which the employee has no independent claim. In many cases, however, arbitrators have encouraged or permitted informal participation by employees who might be affected by the arbitration award, and the AAA Rules specifically allow attendance by any person with a direct interest in the arbitration. (Appendix 2, Rule 22.)

Where an employee can show that the union will not provide fair representation, he may be entitled to separate representation and participation as a matter of law. A few courts have held as much, but such cases are rare and proof would be difficult in any event. The NLRB has adopted a broader rule, that individuals should have the right to separate representation whenever their interests do not coincide with those of the union. Where separate representation has been denied the Board has refused to defer to the subsequent award. The Board's position has had little effect because only a small percentage of arbitrations involve potential unfair labor practices and because both arbitrators and parties dislike the idea of a trilateral arbitration. In addition to the union's interest in maintaining its position as exclusive representative, there is a fear that employee intervention would lead to confusion and disruption.

A related problem involves conflicts between two unions and a single employer. This happens most often in work-assignment disputes where each union claims a contractual right to certain work. Separate arbitrations might lead to equally valid but directly conflicting awards. In just such a case, *Carey v. Westinghouse Electric Corp.*, 375 U.S. 261 (1964), the Supreme Court held that the employer could not refuse to arbitrate simply because of that possibility.

Obviously a single arbitration involving both unions would minimize the problem. (It would not always eliminate it because the two contracts might in fact contain conflicting but equally valid provisions.) If one union rejects such a suggestion may the arbitrator nevertheless require, invite, or permit participation by another union? Arbitrators have differed on each of these possibilities and there have been few court rulings. The Second Circuit Court of Appeals resolved one such dispute by ordering consolidation of two pending arbitrations, but its action has not been repeated elsewhere. *Columbia Broadcasting System, Inc. v. American Recording and Broadcasting Association,* 414 F.2d 1326 (2d Cir. 1969).

3. *Confrontation and Cross-Examination*

A fundamental tenet of our criminal justice system is that the accused must be allowed to confront his accusers and to cross-examine their testimony. The underlying basis of that principle, that the truth of a statement can be determined more accurately when it is subject to the rigors of the adversarial process, is so compelling that it has had a considerable influence on civil law as well as criminal.

It has also influenced arbitration. The problem comes up almost exclusively in one of four contexts: hearsay generally, and evidence coming from customers, fellow employees or professional "spotters." Each of these deserves brief discussion.

(a) *Hearsay.* Hearsay will be dealt with in more detail below, along with other evidentiary questions. For the moment it is sufficient to note that arbitrators almost universally accept hearsay evidence when there is any sort of reasonable explanation why first-hand testimony is not feasible. At the same time, they moderate the risks by evaluating hearsay more critically than other sorts of evidence. Perhaps the most common statement from arbitrators on hearsay is the evidentiary ruling "I'll admit it for what it is worth," carrying the implication that it may not be worth very much.

(b) *Customers, Co-employees and "Spotters."* Employers are understandably reluctant to put any of these three categories of witnesses on the stand even when their testimony is absolutely crucial. An employer may take disciplinary action against an employee following customer complaints but may feel that calling the customer to testify would discourage patronage or at least discourage such complaints. Calling an employee witness may lead to strife within the bargaining unit that neither party wants, and the effectiveness of "spotters" (employees who pose as customers to watch for employee misconduct) would be drastically reduced if their identity became known. Yet in each of these cases the disciplined employee certainly has good reason to want the opportunity to cross-examine the witness.

Faced with these conflicting arguments, arbitrators tend to require the testimony of employee witnesses notwithstanding potential strife, but not the testimony of customers or spotters. In those latter cases, arbitrators have been known to suggest compromises such as private investigation by the arbitrator alone, acceptance of the proffered hearsay evidence subject to the right of the union representative to verify its accuracy privately with the witness, or testimony of the "spotter" behind a screen. Several contracts in industries where these types of cases are frequent spell out procedures to be used and that is obviously the most desirable way to resolve the problem. Absent agreement, compromises along this line seem preferable to simple admission or exclusion of otherwise relevant evidence.

4. *Discovery*

In most cases parties willingly exchange relevant information about pending grievances in the belief that by doing so a settlement may be reached. A union might decide not to take a case to arbitration, for example, if the employer shows sufficient evidence to convince the union it could not win. Or an employer might compromise on a discipline case if the union's evidence seems sufficient to make an arbitrator doubt whether the employee was guilty of the offense charged.

There are many cases where information is not so willingly exchanged. The parties might simply be too suspicious of one another to communicate much, or they might want to reserve some information to use as a "knockout punch" in the arbitration. In still other cases there may be extraneous reasons to withhold the information—to protect the privacy of those who submit comments on employee work performance, for example, or to avoid disclosure of a trade secret.

Unlike criminal or civil litigation there are no pre-hearing discovery procedures in most arbitrations. Some state laws give arbitrators the power of subpoena and provide for depositions (See Sections 7(a) and (b) of the proposed Uniform Arbitration Act, Appendix 7) but this is quite rare. Refusal to provide information may be an unfair labor practice, but NLRB procedures move at a snail's pace.

Once the hearing has begun, a party may ask the arbitrator to order the other side to release relevant information. Usually an arbitrator's order to that effect is honored by the reluctant party, and conceivably it could be enforced in a Section 301 action if it is based on some provision of the contract. In the event it is not obeyed, the arbitrator may draw an inference against the party refusing to produce the evidence. Where the objection to release is based on some plausible concern for confidentiality, the arbitrator may be able to resolve the problem by personally excising irrelevant information or by placing strict limitations on the persons to whom the information may be shown or the uses to which it may be put.

[*122*]

5. Self-Incrimination

Invocation of a claimed Fifth Amendment right against self-incrimination is most frequent where discipline has been administered for conduct that may also be illegal. The employee's position in such a case is most difficult, and his desire not to testify understandable. The claim is sometimes raised in less compelling circumstances, where no criminal conduct is alleged but where the employee would for some other reason like to refuse to testify. Arbitrators seldom possess subpoena power and have no power to punish for contempt, so the question is not one of actually compelling testimony. They can and frequently do draw adverse conclusions from a failure to testify, though, and that is often why the Fifth Amendment is pleaded: in criminal cases such negative inferences are not to be drawn. Moreover, employers may attempt to discipline an employee not for the conduct about which he refuses to testify, but for the refusal itself, as when the employee refuses to cooperate in an investigation of pilferage.

Arbitrators have rejected the notion that the constitutional right is binding on private sector employment problems, but a few have indicated that it represents a desirable policy and have therefore refused to draw any negative inferences from failure to testify. More often they are likely to draw such inferences, particularly where there is no risk of a subsequent criminal proceeding. This has prompted one distinguished arbitrator to suggest rules to govern these cases. Briefly, those rules would allow the arbitrator in a discipline case to draw an adverse inference if an employee declines to testify after having been warned that such an inference might be drawn, but would require that the penalty be sustained only if supported by other evidence against the grievant. This approach strikes a balance that would protect legitimate employee concerns without importing into arbitration concepts having little relevance to labor relations.

6. *Search and Seizure*

In the wake of court decisions establishing an exclusionary rule in criminal cases for improperly obtained evidence, arbitrators have been asked on many occasions to sustain objections to the introduction of such evidence.

Arbitrators have universally upheld the use of evidence obtained in searches pursuant to reasonable work rules, such as routine inspection of handbags and lunchboxes on leaving the plant. With only slightly lower frequency arbitrators have upheld searches of company property such as lockers even if an employee has temporary exclusive use of that property. In both types of cases arbitrators have upheld discipline levied for refusal to permit such searches. Even here the employer would be on stronger ground if the search is pursuant to a published rule. On the other hand, arbitrators have divided on the admissibility of evidence obtained in an *ad hoc* search of an employee's person or property. A majority would probably admit such evidence except in the most blatant cases of invasion of privacy, but a strong minority would restrict management searches to those permitted by reasonable work rules.

7. *Ex Parte Hearings*

Upon occasion one party to an arbitration agreement refuses to participate in the hearing. Obviously the agreement to arbitrate would be worthless if the process could be so easily stymied, so in some circumstances *ex parte* hearings and awards are permitted. The rules of the AAA (Appendix 2, Rule 27) state the requirements for *ex parte* arbitration:

> Unless the law provides to the contrary, the arbitration may proceed in the absence of any party, who, after due notice, fails to be present or fails to obtain an adjournment. An award shall not be made solely on the default of a party. The Arbitrator shall require the other party to submit such evidence as he may require for the making of an award.

Rule 27 is not intended to be used in cases of simple tardiness. The better course of action in that situation would be rescheduling of the hearing. Even in cases of absolute refusal to participate, an *ex parte* hearing is certainly not a very desirable way to resolve grievances, but so long as the contract provides a method of selecting an arbitrator if one party fails to participate, or if the parties have mutually selected an arbitrator before one of them withdraws from participation, the arbitrator so selected does not lose his authority. Where there is no provision for arbitrator selection except by mutual agreement, one party cannot on its own appoint an arbitrator and conduct an *ex parte* hearing; the appropriate remedy in such a case would be a Section 301 action to force the participation of the reluctant party.

8. *Changed Issues, Arguments or Evidence*

In theory the grievance process is supposed to weed out weak cases and focus the issues in those cases taken to arbitration. It works this way in most cases, but it is not uncommon for a party to raise at the hearing or in a post-hearing brief an issue, argument or piece of evidence not considered in the grievance procedure. An employer who discharged employee A for drunkenness might later cite insubordination as the reason; a union that challenged subcontracting as violation of the recognition clause might suddenly assert instead that it was prohibited by past practice; or either party might offer the testimony of a surprise witness unknown to the other party.

Resolution of these problems will differ depending upon the wording of the particular contract or the type of arbitration system established (a permanent umpire may have more flexibility than an *ad hoc* arbitrator with no previous knowledge of the parties or continuing role in their relationship) but some general rules can be stated. Few arbitrators would allow presentation of an entirely new grievance, for instance, because of the deleterious effect this would have on the grievance procedure and because of the inequity of forcing the other party to respond to a new issue without adequate time to prepare. Similarly most arbitrators would hold an employer to the grounds for discharge given at the time it was made, even if other grounds would have been equally valid.

Where the problem is simply that neither party has clearly defined the issues during the grievance procedure, arbitrators are likely to be more tolerant. The arbitrator's concern should be simply to conduct a fair hearing on the issues raised; this may require a recess or continuance to allow the surprised party to prepare for an issue it had not expected to meet, but should seldom require a limitation on the arguments made.

If the problem is one of new evidence rather than new issues or arguments the same considerations should apply. Neither party should be prohibited from presenting newly-discovered evidence even though the better policy would be to disclose such evidence to the other party prior to the hearing. At most the surprised party should be given time to evaluate and respond. Where one party has deliberately withheld important evidence, some arbitrators would ban the new evidence permanently while others perceive only the "surprise" issue and react accordingly.

The equities change somewhat when the new argument or evidence is raised after the hearing. While an arbitrator will be likely to grant a request to reopen a hearing to receive new evidence not previously available, he would not easily consider new evidence simply included in a post-hearing brief. A new argument in a brief presents a more difficult problem. So long as the other party receives a copy of the brief and could, if it wished, submit a reply to the new argument, many arbitrators would have no difficulty with the case. Others would feel some obligation to ask the other party for comment, particularly if he feels he is likely to rely on the new argument in his decision. Few would totally refuse to consider the new argument if it does not amount to an entirely new issue.

In fact, an arbitrator himself may on review of the record discover a basis for a decision that was not mentioned by either party. Is he free to use his discovery, or should he write to the parties and ask them for comments on his theory? Is he free to develop a stronger case for one side than it could for itself? There is simply no generally accepted answer to this dilemma. Common sense dictates that if the contract clause or theory that is "discovered" by the arbitrator is only an arguable solution, he ought not rely on it without asking the parties for comments. On the other hand, most arbitrators do not feel that their role is limited by the imagination of counsel for the parties. Bad representation should not require a bad decision.

9. *The Agreed Case*

"Agreed" cases, those where the parties are not actually in dispute about the desired result but wish it to be announced as if it were the product of arbitration rather than negotiations, pose difficult conceptual problems for the arbitrator. On the one hand, simple acceptance of the parties' wishes makes the hearing a sham, but on the other hand the main purpose of arbitration is to facilitate peaceful resolution of disputes.

There are several reasons why the parties might pose an agreed case to an arbitrator. The most common explanation and the least questionable, is political: the union leaders might understand that a certain result is "right" but may not be able to sell it to the membership on their own authority. This happens from time to time with wage negotiations in weak companies. The union leadership may come to share management's fear that a sizeable wage increase would make the company uncompetitive, with bankruptcy a real possibility, but may be faced with serious pressures from vocal elements within the union that are simply unwilling to listen to any such arguments. Or the union leadership might be forced to challenge the discharge of a popular employee even though it believes him guilty of the offense charged.

There are less honorable, and fortunately less common reasons for agreed cases, too. Again they are likely to be political. The employer and the officers of the union might both desire to get rid of a dissident employee. When the employer discharges him, the union might be forced to take the case to arbitration only to let the arbitrator know by one means or another that they would just as soon lose this one.

Arbitrators differ in their reactions to requests for such "consent awards." In the wage example, many would have no problem so long as the agreement reached by the parties seemed to the arbitrator to be reasonable in the particular context. In individual grievance cases, there is more of a problem because of the very obvious possibility that the union's interests might conflict with those of the grievant.

The Code of Professional Responsibility for Arbitrators of Labor-Management Disputes (Appendix 5, paragraphs 65 and 66) recognizes the ambivalent nature of consent awards by authorizing them only where the arbitrator is convinced that the result is fair and by placing on the arbitrator the responsibility for making sure that all relevant information is disclosed:

I. CONSENT AWARDS

1.   Prior to issuance of an award, the parties may jointly request the arbitrator to include in the award certain agreements between them, concerning some or all of the issues.   If the arbitrator believes that a suggested award is proper, fair, sound, and lawful, it is consistent with professional responsibility to adopt it.

a.   Before complying with such a request, an arbitrator must be certain that he or she understands the suggested settlement adequately in order to be able to appraise its terms.   If it appears that pertinent facts or circumstances may not have been disclosed, the arbitrator should take the initiative to assure that all significant aspects of the case are fully understood.   To this end, the arbitrator may request additional specific information and may question witnesses at a hearing.

[*131*]

C. THE BURDEN OF PROOF

The term "burden of proof" actually comprises several distinct burdens, the burden of producing evidence, the burden of persuasion, and the burden of establishing a sufficient quantum of proof.

1. *The Burden of Producing Evidence*

Logic and custom dictate that in arbitration as in court the moving party should normally bear the burden of producing some evidence to support its position. In legal terms, the moving party is expected to establish a *prima facie* case, that is, sufficient evidence to convince the trier of fact of the rightness of the party's cause if no refutation is made by the other. Once it does so, the burden of producing evidence shifts to the other party, which must refute the *prima facie* case or lose the dispute. If the moving party cannot establish a *prima facie* case it will lose the dispute even if the other party remains mute. It should be noted that this burden may shift from one party to the other as the issue under discussion changes. A union claiming a seniority violation would have the initial burden of proceeding, for example, but if the employer justified its action by reference to federal law granting veterans certain re-employment rights, the burden of presenting evidence on that question would shift to the employer.

Custom has established one major exception to this rule. In discipline cases the employer is almost uniformly required by the arbitrator to proceed first and show the justification for the discipline imposed. It is not clear how or why this exception arose. The most common explanations are that in such cases management precipitated the action leading to the grievance and that the employer is likely to have a greater command of the pertinent facts and records. Especially with regard to discharges, one also hears the suggestion that management should properly bear the burden because of the serious harm erroneously imposed discipline can cause the employee. The trouble with these explanations is that they are equally true of many other kinds of cases (layoffs and automation, for example) where the arbitrator would never think of asking the employer to proceed first.

2. *The Burden of Persuasion*

The question of which party is to present its case first would hardly be worth arguing if the parties did not see it as reflecting the placing of the burden of persuasion. If the evidence presented is equally balanced, which side prevails? The perception of the parties is for the most part correct. Although some arbitrators hesitate to state which side must carry the burden, most would in practice place it on the same party bearing the burden of going forward.

This means that in most cases the union as moving party must establish the sufficiency of its position or lose the case. It means as well that management must generally prove that there is "just cause" for disciplinary action, and that any party seeking to establish some decisive fact (waiver of a contract right, supersession of the agreement by state or federal law, or the excessiveness of the penalty imposed for some admitted offense) must persuade the arbitrator of that fact.

3. The Quantum of Proof

There are three levels of proof that can be demanded of a party bearing the burden of persuasion: proof beyond a reasonable doubt, proof by "clear and convincing" evidence, and proof by a preponderance of the evidence.

The first of these, proof beyond a reasonable doubt, is the standard applied in criminal trials and, as might be expected, is imposed in arbitration only in the most serious cases, usually discharges for offenses constituting criminal conduct or demonstrating moral turpitude. The explanation for imposition of this strict standard is that discharge for such reasons will brand an employee for life just as severely as would a criminal conviction for the same charges. Other arbitrators reject the criminal law analogy. They note that because of the liberal application of evidentiary rules in arbitration no one could fairly assume that an arbitrator's decision to uphold a discharge is as conclusive of the facts as the verdict of a

[134]

jury, and that even the courts themselves only impose the "preponderance of the evidence" standard in civil cases, even when commission of a crime is directly in issue. A civil suit for assault or intentional conversion of property could be won on the lesser standard, for example, and there is no strong reason to require the higher standard in arbitration, which is only another, non-governmental form of civil litigation.

The middle standard, proof by "clear and convincing" evidence, is applied most frequently in discharge cases not involving criminal conduct or moral turpitude and in cases alleging serious misconduct by the company such as discrimination because of union activity. Arbitrators tend to view these cases as being more serious than most and thus require a stricter standard. Just how much evidence it takes to meet the "clear and convincing" test is of course hard to pin down.

The least severe standard, proof by a preponderance of the evidence, is the most commonly applied. In addition to those cases explicitly using it, many that contain no discussion of the appropriate standard seem to apply this one. It has the virtue of being the easiest to use, for the arbitrator need only ask which case seems the stronger, or which version of the facts is more likely to be true.

D. SOME PROBLEMS OF EVIDENCE

1. The Applicability of Evidentiary Rules to Arbitration

The AAA rules provide that "The Arbitrator shall be the judge of the relevance and materiality of the evidence offered and conformity to legal rules of evidence shall not be necessary" (Appendix 2, Rule 28). There are many reasons why evidentiary rules are not strictly applied in labor arbitration. For one thing, arbitration is intended to be a simple, informal procedure that frequently will not involve a single lawyer; rigid adherence to technical rules would obviously conflict with those intentions. Second, many of the legal rules of evidence were developed to protect lay juries from prejudicial or unreliable testimony or exhibits and are therefore inapplicable to administrative tribunals and, perforce, to arbitrations. To the contrary, most arbitrators are eager to learn all that they can about the situation before them and believe that evidence which might not be admissible in court may help them learn. If it turns out not to be helpful or reliable, it can always be ignored. Third, many arbitrators believe that there is a "therapeutic value" to testimony, that the parties benefit when witnesses get something "off their chests" even if that something has no probative value to the issues in the arbitration. Fourth, as a practical matter an arbitrator's award will not be overturned no matter how liberal his evidentiary rulings might be, as least so long as he does not base his award on obviously irrelevant or erroneous evidence. Refusal to hear relevant evidence, on the other hand, may constitute grounds for overturning the award. To recognize that legal rules of evidence are not binding in arbitration is not to say that they are irrelevant. They are in fact useful in several different ways. The AAA rule quoted above recognizes that arbitrators must make judgments about materiality and relevance and should not allow introduction of obviously immaterial, irrelevant or redundant testimony; the rules of evidence developed in centuries of litigation may help him decide those issues. Even if he does admit questionable evidence, legal rules of evidence may assist him in deciding how much weight it should have. The reasons courts distrust hearsay evidence, for example, (likelihood of errors in reporting and the absence of cross-examination), should warn the arbitrator not to place too much reliance upon it. The careful advocate will point out the unreliability of evidence in the course of an objection to it even if he knows that his objection will not be sustained. Finally, the arbitrator has an obligation to conduct an orderly proceeding that will lead him to a resolution of the issues before him. Implicit in this obligation is a duty not to allow the proceeding to wander too far afield, drag on interminably or be influenced by prejudicial or unreliable testimony. The rules of evidence, flexibly applied, can help to fulfill those obligations without unduly curtailing the rights of the parties to establish their cases.

The following sections deal with the major evidentiary issues in labor arbitration.

2. *Hearsay*

Hearsay is second-hand evidence, *i. e.*, evidence not of what the witness knows but of what he heard another say, which is offered to prove the truth of what was said. Courts tend to exclude it because of the risk of inaccuracy in the repetition and because there is no opportunity to cross-examine the person making the original statement. The rule excluding hearsay is riddled with exceptions which recognize either an unusual degree of reliability (*e. g.*, business records and testimony from a previous hearing or another suit) or a particular need for the testimony (*e. g.*, dying declarations).

Hearsay is generally admitted in arbitration, although frequently with the qualification that the arbitrator will consider it only "for what it's worth." In addition to the generally liberal application of evidentiary rules, the admission of hearsay in arbitration can be explained by the desire of all concerned for simple proceedings: informality and speed would be hard to maintain if

[*138*]

hearsay were not admitted, for more witnesses would be needed, there would have to be more careful preparation, and the complexity of the hearsay rules would require an even greater use of lawyers than at present.

It may therefore be necessary to admit hearsay, but recognizing its unreliability arbitrators tend to require corroboration of important points and to give hearsay little weight where the opposing party presents contradictory evidence that is subject to cross-examination.

Affidavits are a type of hearsay evidence the admission of which is explicitly authorized by AAA rules (Appendix 2, Rule 29). That rule cautions that the arbitrator shall give an affidavit "only such weight as he deems proper after consideration of any objections made to its admission."

3. *Parol Evidence*

The "parol evidence rule" prohibits the use of evidence of prior or contemporaneous oral agreements or of prior written agreements to vary the terms of a written contract which, on its face, is integrated and complete. (Note that it has nothing to do with **subsequent** agreements, whether concluded orally, in writing or by conduct.) Contracts frequently contain their own exclusionary rule by stating that all agreements between the parties are contained therein and that modifications are valid only when

[*139*]

in writing and signed by both parties. The rule is thus closely related to the jurisdiction of the arbitrator: a party asserting the rule claims, in effect, that the arbitrator's power extends only to an interpretation of the written contract. Evidence challenged under the parol evidence rule may be offered in an attempt to reform the contract, to clarify an ambiguity, or to establish the existence of a collateral agreement.

Most but by no means all of the arbitration authorities agree that an arbitrator may consider evidence showing that the apparent terms of a contract do not accurately reflect the agreement between the parties. Parol evidence indicating that a typist or printer erroneously recorded the parties' intent would be admitted to reform the agreement, for example. The reasoning behind this approach is clear enough. The arbitrator's task is to interpret the contract **as the parties intended it**—if the document is not a correct statement of their intentions, he must follow the true agreement rather than the false one.

On the other hand, virtually all authorities agree that parol evidence should not be entertained to vary terms that are clear and unambiguous. This is little help, however, for the question is never raised when both parties agree on the meaning of "clear and unambiguous" language, and even if the meaning seems clear to an outsider at least one party to a dispute can be counted on to argue that it is not. As a practical matter an arbitrator cannot even make a ruling on whether the language is unambiguous without hearing the proffered evidence, and it is surely admissible for that purpose. If he finds no ambiguity the evidence should be ignored, but if he does find it ambiguous the evidence may be considered to resolve the ambiguity.

If the parol evidence rule has any force at all in arbitration, it is with regard to evidence of prior or contemporaneous agreements on subjects covered in the contract itself. Leaving aside for the moment past practices conflicting with or adding to the agreement, most arbitrators would not rely on oral agreements to change the terms of the agreement, for to do so would destroy the parties' confidence in the stability of the written document. Prior or contemporaneous *written* agreements present more difficult cases. If such agreements are on subjects included in the main contract, they should not be allowed to vary the contract terms. If they deal with matters not intended to be covered by the contract they may well be valid, but at least in the case of a standard arbitration clause, the arbitrator may have no authority to apply them, for the dispute would not turn on the interpretation or application of the contract creating the arbitration.

In summary, arbitrators seem to pay the parol evidence rule no more attention than do the courts. It has little force as a rule of admissibility for there are numerous exceptions to the rule, but it does seem to have some influence in so far as it cautions the arbitrator to limit his role to the interpretation of the contract from which he receives his authority.

4. *Past Practice*

Justice Douglas stated in the *Steelworkers Trilogy* that

> The labor arbitrator's source of law is not confined to the express provisions of the contract, as the industrial common law—the practices of the industry and the shop—is equally a part of the collective bargaining agreement although not expressed in it.

This doctrine poses a problem related to but broader than the parol evidence question. It is broader because it deals with assertions of subsequent agreements as well as prior or contemporaneous ones. Like parol evidence generally, past practice can be offered to resolve an ambiguity, to fill a gap where the contract is silent, or to supplement or contradict apparently clear language.

(a) *Establishment of a Past Practice*. Arbitrators agree that a party asserting a past practice bears the burden of establishing the existence of that practice. This burden can be met by showing that the parties regarded some action as the normal, proper and exclusive response to a particular situation. Several factors can be examined to determine whether such an understanding exists. The most important of these is **mutuality**, which can be either express or implied, as by a continued failure to object to a course of conduct that is open and repeated. Almost any form of objection may be cited to disprove mutuality, such as occasional reprimands to employees who engage in the practice or a complaint from a union representative to a responsible company official.

Second, the asserted practice should be **clear and consistent**. Ambiguity about the content of a practice reveals the lack of understanding that certain conduct was the normal and proper response to a particular situation, and inconsistency demonstrates that there was not a single past practice but two or more.

Third, the practice should be of some significant **frequency and duration**. A single prior incident might constitute a past practice if the circumstances giving rise to it are unlikely to be repeated and there was no objection to the conduct in that one instance, but cases of this sort are rare. Most arbitrators would insist on several instances of the conduct in question, and would give weight to the conduct in proportion to its frequency and duration.

Finally, at least some arbitrators would require that the party asserting the practice show that it was **not a simple gratuity**. They would, in other words, not force an employer to continue some act of good will that was never intended to become a binding term. A cash bonus, paid only by special order of the Board of Directors after a year of particularly high profits would not become a binding past practice without more; but a routine gift of a Thanksgiving turkey might, if regularly repeated.

Discussions during contract negotiations are often looked at as evidence of the existence or non-existence of a past practice. This can be misleading, particularly when such discussions do not result in language in the contract. A clear promise to continue a practice or vigorous opposition to formalizing a benefit in the contract may cast some light on the intentions of the parties, though.

(b) *Use of a Past Practice.* Once the existence of a consistent past practice is established, the arbitrator must decide what effect it is to have. The best way to resolve that issue is through the contract itself. A clear statement that all past practices constituting a benefit to employees are to be deemed incorporated in the contract will be honored by arbitrators, as will a comparably clear statement that no past practice is to be considered binding unless spelled out in the contract. General language may be insufficient, however. Several arbitrators have held that broad management rights clauses or statements that the written document constitutes the "entire agreement" between

[*144*]

the parties will not negate a practice that the parties have intended to be binding.

In the absence of any contract provision on the effect of past practices, arbitrators have used them in many different ways. The most widely accepted use is to **clarify ambiguous language.** Almost as common is the use of past practices to **implement general language** such as "just cause" for discharge or "relatively equal ability" for promotion.

More controversial is the use of past practice to **supplement a silent contract.** Some arbitrators believe that written agreements are generally intended to be complete and that neither party should be burdened with any implied obligations. At the opposite pole are those who regard all past practices not in conflict with the contract to be incorporated in it, *sub silentio.* The latter view is well expressed by the quote from Justice Douglas at the beginning of this section.

Most difficult of all is the assertion of past practice to **contradict apparently unambiguous contract language.** Traditional contract law frowns upon such use of past practice, and many arbitrators take the same position. After all, why would the parties settle on certain language if they did not intend to follow it?

While the traditional approach stands as a caution against ignoring carefully expressed agreements, it should not constitute a rigid barrier to the use of past practice even when that practice conflicts with the written document. Even traditional contract law recognizes that parties may amend their agreements by their actions, at least where the Statute of Frauds is not applicable. Certainly labor agreements should be treated no more strictly in this respect than other contracts. Traditional contract law also assumes the existence of clear and unambiguous language, used in the normal fashion by persons who knew what they were doing. In the collective bargaining context these assumptions may not be valid. Much of the drafting of labor agreements is done in very pressured circumstances by persons with no special gift with the English language. Many contracts use even simple words in peculiar, even inconsistent ways. These factors have prompted one authority to speak of the "inherent ambiguity" of even apparently clear language in collective bargaining agreements and to suggest that it would be inaccurate to take such language at face value. Perhaps a better approach to the use of evidence of a past practice conflicting with contract language is to ask which type of evidence provides the strongest indication of the parties' intentions. In most cases that will be the contract, but where the practice is a better indication it should not be ignored.

(c) *Termination of a Past Practice.* Once a practice has become well enough established to constitute a part of the collective bargaining agreement, it can be terminated only as other parts of that agreement can be terminated. Usually this will mean that mutual agreement is required, but it is important to note that this mutual agreement can be expressed in the same variety of ways that agreement to create a binding past practice can be expressed—in writing, in words, in actions and even in some cases by inaction. In addition, many arbitrators would allow unilateral termination in some circumstances. If a particular practice has been established as a result of a certain manufacturing process, a legitimate change in that process might justify a unilateral change in the practice. The size of a work crew might become a binding practice for instance, but introduction of a new machine might make it possible to reduce crew size with no extra burden on the remaining crew members; many arbitrators would find the reduction permissible in the absence of a written restriction.

5. *Past Employee Conduct*

Whether evidence of an employee's past conduct is admissible is primarily a question of relevancy. Certain past conduct may be highly relevant to the grievance and therefore readily admissible. Other conduct may show nothing about the merits of the current grievance and would either be denied admission or, if admitted, would be given no weight. Admissibility thus depends on the nature and time of the conduct offered as evidence and on the specific question for which it is offered.

In any case, evidence of past misconduct will generally be considered only when it involves proved offenses of which the employee had notice. To allow use of other sorts of past misconduct would force the grievant to defend himself against stale charges which might serve only to prejudice the current case. Evidence of satisfactory past conduct is more liberally accepted although it may be given little weight if it does not bear directly on the current grievance.

Evidence of past misconduct may be offered (a) to justify the degree of penalty imposed, as when the employer shows that progressive discipline has not corrected some recurring problem; (b) to suggest the likelihood that the employee actually committed the offense with which he is charged; or (c) to undermine the credibility of the employee as a witness.

Evidence offered for the first purpose, to justify the degree of penalty imposed, is usually admitted, but whether it has any impact will depend on the relationship between the offenses and the period of time involved. Evidence of serious absenteeism in recent months may explain a discharge because of absenteeism, for example, but the same record would hardly be relevant if it was several years old with no recent problem. Similarly, evidence of insubordination would not be very helpful in deciding whether the discharge for absenteeism was appropriate. Some arbitrators suggest that a strict standard ought to be applied for evidence of prior misconduct, but it is hard to square this approach with the universal acceptance of a record of good conduct. One would seem to be as relevant as the other, and no more.

The criminal law is an inexact analogy, but it does provide a good basis for comparison on this matter. Speaking very generally, records of past convictions are usually accepted after conviction and prior to sentencing, but not for the purpose of indicating guilt on the current charge. Presumably this distinction reflects the belief that a judge is less likely to be prejudiced by such information than a jury, and a further belief that the sentence ought to fit the individual as well as the crime while the determination of guilt should rest solely upon the facts presented. Arbitration does not lend itself to this division of labor. The arbitrator is both judge and jury and must receive evidence on all matters before making any decision. Then, too, the arbitrator normally sits in review of management's decision and does not have the broad discretion possessed by a sentencing judge.

These differences between arbitration and the criminal law do not fully explain the fact that arbitrators not only admit evidence of past misconduct but often treat it as having significant probative value on the question of guilt. Again, the weight given to such evidence will depend on the time period involved and on whether or not the earlier offenses are "functionally related" to the latter. If those tests (and the requirement that the earlier offenses were made known to the employee) are met, most arbitrators would be willing to assume that an employee who had ignored orders in the past might have done so again and that an employee previously disciplined for reporting to work intoxicated was more likely to have done so again as charged than to have been, as he claimed, simply tired. The possible harshness of this rule is mitigated by the requirement of most arbitrators that there be some independent evidence of the offense charged. Past misconduct, in other words, is not conclusive of current behavior though it may be relevant evidence on this point.

Finally, evidence of past misconduct is sometimes offered to undermine a witness' credibility. A common example of this is the introduction of evidence of prior criminal convictions notwithstanding pleas of not guilty to suggest that a current denial is not to be given much weight.

Most arbitrators would accept such evidence as long as it is not offered simply to prejudice the arbitration. It is unclear how much weight it would be given, or whether its influence would be limited to the credibility issue.

A different problem is presented when evidence of misconduct is offered in non-discipline cases. The issue comes up in this context most frequently in promotion cases when the senior employee is passed over because of a bad record. Most of these disputes turn on the wording of the particular contract. When the wording does not indicate whether past conduct is relevant to promotion decisions, arbitrators differ in their rulings. Some deny the admissibility of instances of past misconduct because it does not bear on the grievant's ability to perform the work in the higher classification. This was the ruling in one case where the misconduct involved extraordinary absenteeism and the job in question was crucial to work performed by many other employees. The arbitrator rejected the employer's claim that the grievant lacked the ability to perform the job because he might not show up for it; the evidence was clear that he knew how to perform the work, the arbitrator said, and thus possessed the requisite ability. The employer could punish future absenteeism appropriately if it occurred. Other arbitrators are much more willing to consider any evidence bearing on the grievant's fitness for the job.

6. *Polygraph Evidence*

The polygraph, or "lie detector" as it is more commonly known, operates on the premise that lying causes measurable changes in pulse, blood pressure or respiration. The machine measures these physiological activities during questioning, and a trained operator is said to be able to interpret the graphs to detect lies. The polygraph is a widely-used tool of personnel management, particularly in employment interviews and security investigations where theft is a serious problem.

The reliability of polygraph evidence is a matter of some dispute among those who have studied the question. Some critics attack the fundamental premise, arguing that the machine at most measures emotional state, not truth or falsity. Others point out that much depends on the examiner himself and that many examiners lack the thorough training required for any degree of accuracy. Even proponents of the polygraph admit that it is accurate in only 75–80% of the cases.

Because of the lack of any consensus in the scientific community about the reliability of the polygraph, criminal courts uniformly reject polygraph evidence absent a stipulation to its reliability. This is true regardless of which side seeks to introduce the evidence. For the same reason courts also refuse to allow any inference to be drawn from the witness' willingness or unwillingness to take a polygraph exam. Several states have gone beyond such evidentiary rules and have passed laws forbidding employers from requiring employees to submit to lie detector tests.

The polygraph presents two issues to arbitrators. The first is whether refusal to submit to a polygraph exam constitutes just cause for discipline or discharge. The second is whether evidence of a completed polygraph exam is admissible and if so, how much weight it should be given.

With very few exceptions, arbitrators have held that employers may not punish an employee for failure to take a lie detector test. The exceptions to this general rule have occurred chiefly (a) where other evidence of some offense points to a small number of employees and it is difficult if not impossible to determine which in the small group are the true offenders, or (b) where the collective bargaining contract requires guards to cooperate fully in the investigation of thefts. More general "cooperation" clauses and individual promises to take a polygraph exam on the request of the employer have not been regarded in arbitration as binding.

Nor do arbitrators give much weight to polygraph results, even where the test has been taken voluntarily. Many arbitrators would reject such evidence summarily because of its lack of reliability although like the courts they would probably accept the evidence if the parties stipulated to its introduction. Even when such evidence is admitted, it is given little weight. At most, arbitrators treat polygraph data as corroborative of other evidence of guilt or innocence.

One commentator has suggested that at least four conditions should be met for polygraph tests to be admissible: (a) the examiner should be qualified; (b) the test should be administered promptly after the incident being investigated; (c) the test should be voluntary; and (d) the examiner should be available for cross-examination, with his records. It is clear that even higher standards would be required before polygraph evidence would be given decisive weight.

7. *Medical Testimony*

Medical testimony is most frequently offered in cases where the employer has refused to allow an employee to perform certain work (or, frequently, any work at all) because of doubts about the employee's physical fitness. Three separate issues should be mentioned: (a) the propriety of an employer's requirement of clearance by its medical officer; (b) the use of written statements rather than oral medical testimony; and (c) resolution of conflicts in medical testimony.

Where the contract is silent, employer imposition of a medical clearance requirement is likely to be challenged as a unilateral change in working conditions or as an unreasonable restriction on employees. Arbitrators have had little sympathy for such claims. Where the medical problem at issue involves any potential harm to the employee himself or to his co-workers, arbitrators have upheld requirements of medical clearances, concentrating instead on whether the procedure used was fair and the ultimate decision reasonable.

Practical considerations, most importantly the cost and scheduling difficulties involved in requiring doctors to testify in person, have dictated the answer to the problem of "hearsay" medical testimony. Absent contractual agreement to the contrary, arbitrators will accept written statements or affidavits from doctors. A written statement may well be given less weight than an identical statement made in person and subject to cross-examination, but still may carry great weight, particularly if the opposing side offers no medical testimony at all. The weight accorded to such statements will of course be reduced where there is conflicting evidence of any type.

It is impossible to describe a simple way for arbitrators to resolve conflicts of medical testimony. The role of the arbitrator in such cases is like that of a lay jury presented with conflicting expert testimony of any sort. He, like the jury, must decide between the experts using his own critical analysis of the evidence, his perception of the relative credibility of the witnesses, and certain helpful presumptions. The most important presumption is that a decision by the employer based on medical advice will be assumed valid unless it is rebutted by the grievant or is shown to be arbitrary, capricious, discriminatory or based on inadequate data. Some arbitrators further qualify this presumption by insisting that the employer must act in complete good faith and must provide the grievant fair opportunity to overcome its medical officer's views before reaching a final decision. With the consent of the parties, the arbitrator could consult with a doctor of his own choosing to evaluate the medical testimony, but this rarely happens.

If the issue is still in doubt after application of this presumption, common sense dictates a few additional rules-of-thumb: greater weight will be given to the evidence of a specialist, a doctor who has had extensive first-hand opportunity to examine the grievant, or an expert who has recently examined the grievant, than to evidence from a generalist, a doctor relying on second-hand data, or one who made a diagnosis some time ago. In addition, a precise statement keyed to the demands of the job in question will be more helpful than a general comment on the grievant's over-all health.

E. THE ROLE OF ARBITRAL PRECEDENT

Past arbitration awards are not legally binding on an arbitrator no matter how similar they might be to the instant situation, parties and issues. They may carry some influence, however, and the purpose of this section is to explore the nature and extent of this influence.

Many commentators deplore the very notion of arbitral precedent. To them it smacks of rigid legalism, of a slavish adherence to past decisions which becomes an end in itself to the detriment of flexibility, informality and even justice. They fear that if the doctrine is allowed to gain a foothold it will develop into an exaggerated form of *stare decisis,* with far less justification for its existence in arbitration than in the courts of law.

Notwithstanding this criticism, most arbitrators and parties do make some use of past awards. The body of published awards represents the accumulated experience and wisdom of thousands of arbitrators, and careful use of that accumulation can assist labor, management and arbitrators alike. Frequent interpretation of contract language enables parties to use such language in their agreements with reasonable assurance that in the future the language will mean pretty much what it has meant in the past. This is conducive to stable labor relations and discourages frivolous grievances. The body of precedent also guides arbitrators in later cases by providing statements of prevailing rules, standards and meanings. The arbitrator who looks to a settled course of arbitral precedent for guidance will find his own job easier, may benefit in his thinking from views not presented at the hearing, and should be assured that his opinion will not come as a terrible shock to either party. Quite possibly the chance that an award might be published will encourage arbitrators to render carefully considered decisions lest they be embarrassed by a sloppy piece of work.

The usefulness of any prior award will of course depend on its inherent logic and fairness and on the similarity of its terms and facts to the case to which it is applied. Precedential force is always a matter of degree controlled by those factors. Keeping this in mind, it is possible to distinguish between "authoritative" awards which possess a high degree of influence on a later case and "persuasive" awards which are helpful but not in any sense controlling.

Authoritative awards bear a somewhat loose relationship to the legal doctrines of *res judicata* and collateral estoppel, but those terms are too technical to be of much help. Arbitrators, like courts, will refuse to allow the same case (that is, the merits of a dispute arising from a single event or incident) to be relitigated once a final decision has been rendered. The same issue may arise between the parties in a different context, however, involving a new event, a slightly varying fact situation or a new grievant, and it is in such situations that prior awards may exercise greatest influence. Particularly where the parties have indicated a preference for stability and predictability by adopting the permanent umpire system, a clear precedent will govern a later decision on the same issue absent a change in contract language or a showing that the prior decisions were erroneous.

Even *ad hoc* arbitrators tend to view a prior award on the same issue between the same parties as having become part of the contract. The parties may change the arbitrator's holding by negotiation, of course, but if they do not and especially if they subsequently readopt the disputed language without amendment, the arbitrator may reasonably assume that the earlier award accurately stated their intentions.

There is nothing particularly "legalistic" about such holdings and a moment's reflection will indicate the difficulties any other course would present. If every issue could be endlessly relitigated *de novo* in the hope of finding one arbitrator who will disagree with his predecessors, there would be little point to arbitration as a system of dispute resolution. The parties would have no firm guides to future conduct and the grievance process would very likely become clogged with hopeless complaints.

All of this presumes the existence of a clear precedent. Where there are conflicting awards, awards with no supporting opinions, or mere dicta in opinions on other issues there is no such precedent and the arbitrator would be free to strike out on his own.

To a lesser degree a change in parties might undercut the authoritative nature of earlier awards. If a company and union borrow some or all of a contract recently negotiated by other parties, an arbitration decision in a dispute in the first plant would not be very authoritative in a case arising at the second, for each pair of parties might have adopted the language with different intentions. Where one of the parties is the same, as in the case of a new employer signing a master contract previously negotiated by the union with other employers, the newcomer might well be bound by existing arbitral construction of that contract. The very purpose of a master contract is to guarantee similarity in the terms and conditions of employment and most arbitrators would be very hesitant to force inconsistent results on different employers.

The authority of a prior award can always be attacked if the challenging party can show that it was erroneous or that it would be unfair to apply it to the new case. This can be done in any of several different ways. If the earlier opinion is marked by flagrant bias or bad judgment, no arbitrator would feel compelled to follow it. If the prior award was made without the benefit of crucial facts its authority is suspect, and if conditions have changed so substantially that continued adherence would be unreasonable, a different ruling might be expected. But absent such an unusual claim, most arbitrators would be reluctant to upset a well-established rule where the parties themselves have not chosen to do so.

All other awards are more or less persuasive, but not authoritative. A settled course of arbitral decision on a recurring issue, such as whether certain conduct constitutes just cause for discharge, is likely to carry great weight, although the weight may be due more to the inherent logic of the position than to its frequent repetition. In less settled areas, the weight of a particular opinion will depend on the similarity of language and situation and on the logic and equity of the opinion.

To say that a prior award is persuasive does not mean that it is controlling. It may be distinguished or criticized and in any event is merely one of many factors the arbitrator must consider before making his decision.

F. PRINCIPLES OF INTERPRETATION

Apart from the relatively small percentage of cases involving questions of fact, the arbitrator's task is one of interpretation: he must determine just what the parties meant when they adopted certain language, or how they would have wanted their language to be applied in specific circumstances. Standardized contract language and a desire for predictability have caused arbitrators to follow a number of general principles of interpretation in fulfilling this task, of which the following are the most important.

1. *If the Relevant Language is Clear and Unambiguous, It Ought to be Applied as It Appears Without Recourse to Other Indications of Intent*

This is of course simply a restatement of the parol evidence rule discussed above and is subject to the qualifications expressed in that earlier discussion. It is mentioned again because this principle is a rule of interpretation as well as one of admissibility. Because contrary past practice is most often used to counteract the apparent meaning of a contract clause, a corollary principle of interpretation should also be mentioned at this point: clear and unambiguous language prevails over a contrary past practice. This corollary has also been discussed above and for present purposes it should be sufficient to raise one new problem: How does the arbitrator know whether certain language is "clear and unambiguous"? An ambiguity is not created simply because the parties disagree over the meaning of a phrase, for that would only encourage them to argue over the clearest provisions in the hope of a favorable arbitration award. The test most often cited is that there is no ambiguity if the contract is so clear on the issue that the intentions of the parties can be determined using no other guide than the contract itself. This test borders on a tautology, however, for it comes perilously close to a statement that language is unambiguous if it is clear on its face. Perhaps a better way of putting it would be to ask if a single, obvious and reasonable meaning appears from a reading of the language in the context of the rest of the contract. If so, that meaning is to be applied.

It should be pointed out that ambiguities come in at least two different forms. They can be patent or latent. Patent ambiguities are apparent in the language itself; latent ambiguities occur when the language itself seems clear and intelligible but where some extrinsic fact makes the language susceptible of another meaning. A clause providing that the employer may fill "temporary jobs lasting less than 30 days" without going through a bidding procedure seems clear enough standing alone, but is it so clear when the employer relies on it to fill the position of an employee entitled to a personal holiday and that employee would rather work the day for premium pay under another clause entitling him to do just that? Here the second clause is an extrinsic fact that operates to limit the meaning of the first and in so doing shows that the first contains at least one ambiguity.

2. *The Sounds of Silence: Interpretation Without Specific Language*

Arbitrators are frequently faced with difficult questions of interpretation arising from issues that are not addressed in the contract. Two principles are used to resolve many of these questions:

(a) *Evidence of a Consistent Past Practice may be Used to Fill in Gaps and to Supplement the Written Agreement.* This principle is discussed at some length above. It bears reiterating that arbitrators are more inclined to rely on past practice to fill in gaps and to provide definitions than to add new restrictions on management action, although many examples of each can be found in the reports.

(b) *Management Retains all Rights Not Limited by the Collective Bargaining Agreement.* Usually termed the "reserved rights doctrine," this principle is based on the argument that because the employer possessed all rights to run the business before the union came on the scene it must still possess those the union did not succeed in limiting. If this were not so, it would mean either that all such rights passed *sub silentio* to the union or that they simply disappeared, and neither of these possibilities is very reasonable. This principle is still the subject of some dispute in the arbitration community, but a large majority of arbitrators follow it with a few qualifications. One such qualification is an implied "good faith" or "fair dealing" obligation, which simply holds that the employer may not use reserved rights to destroy others specified in the contract. An employer could not use a reserved right to subcontract in a manner that would abolish the bargaining unit for, example. A second important qualification is that the reserved rights principle applies only to situations where **no** contract provision is applicable; it is not a limitation on the application of general language to specific cases. A general seniority clause may or may not require distribution of new equipment to the most senior employees first, but whether it does depends not on the reserved rights principle but on the interpretation of the seniority clause itself. A third qualification is that reserved rights can be limited by a clear past practice unless the contract provides otherwise.

3. An Interpretation that Would Bring the Contract Into Conflict With Positive Law is to be Avoided

We move now into the realm of ambiguous language. The rules that follow are not ranked in any order of importance, but surely this is one of the first that ought to be applied. Some of the potential problems involved in asking arbitrators to rule on legal issues were discussed above in connection with judicial review of awards dealing with claims of race or sex discrimination. It is not necessary to repeat those problems here, for this rule of interpretation is limited to cases involving a recognized conflict with some legal requirement. Where one interpretation would force that conflict and another would avoid it, the latter should be accepted in the absence of truly compelling evidence that the former is the right one.

This principle rests on a presumption few people would question, that parties to contracts intend their agreements to be legal, if for no other reason than to make them legally enforceable. Because no court would enforce an award ordering a party to violate the law, it would be unreasonable to assume that the parties would have wanted such an award.

4. Specific Language is Controlling Over General Language

In this sense "specific language" refers to a provision covering a particular named category of persons or events. The principle simply states that when such a provision exists in possible conflict with more general language that applies to the issue only by implication or extension, the specific provision is presumed to be the one the parties wanted to govern the case. Even specific language can be ambiguous, however, and might require further interpretation.

5. Ambiguous Language Must be Construed in Context

There would be no point in pulling a provision out of the contract and ignoring the rest of the document. The agreement is presumed to be an interrelated, functioning entity, and each clause should be viewed as a part of that entity.

From this observation two more precise rules follow. First, language should be interpreted in a manner that would make it compatible with the rest of the agreement. An interpretation that would nullify some other provision should be avoided, for if the parties intended that result they would not have included the nullified part. Another way of saying this is that a contract should always be interpreted in a fashion that will give effect to all of its parts.

Second, the context may limit general language. If an article of the contract deals with recalls to work after a layoff, a sentence in that article providing that "seniority shall be applied in all cases where the most senior employee has the ability to do the work" should be interpreted to apply only to recalls and not to promotions or other matters.

6. *Words Should be Given Their Normal Meaning Absent Evidence That Some Other Meaning Was Intended*

This principle is an important one, but it can be easily misunderstood. It simply states the assumption that in most cases people use words with their normal meaning in mind and that if they have a special or technical meaning in mind they will give some indication of that intention. (To find the normal meaning of a word, any reliable dictionary may be used.) One implicit qualification of this rule is that the normal meaning should not produce unreasonable consequences. If it does, that fact itself may give good reason to believe that the parties intended the language in a special sense that would produce more reasonable results.

On the other hand, it should be assumed that trade and technical terms were used with their trade or technical meanings in mind unless there is clear evidence that another meaning was intended. (A technical dictionary is just as appropriate for finding a technical definition as a general dictionary is for finding the ordinary meaning of a term.)

7. *Ambiguous Language Should be Construed Against the Drafter*

This principle of interpretation is to be used with care, preferably only when no other rule of construction provides a satisfactory result. It is based on the belief that the drafter can more easily prevent mistakes and should therefore bear the risk of his own ambiguity. Even leaving aside the occasional difficulty in determining whether one side can properly be termed the drafter of language both agreed to, there is another problem with the principle. Many problems of interpretation come up under circumstances that would have been extremely difficult to foresee, and it might not be fair to penalize a drafter for lacking superhuman perspicacity. That is why other principles of interpretation should be tried first. If all else fails, placing the burden on the drafter is probably a little fairer than tossing a coin.

8. *Forfeitures Should be Avoided*

Forfeiture, the loss of a right as a penalty for some fault, is usually provided with some specificity. The conditions under which an employee forfeits his seniority are often carefully listed, for example. Similarly, when failure to comply with procedural steps in the grievance process is intended to work a forfeiture of the right to go to arbitration, the contract will usually say so in relatively clear terms.

It follows from this that forfeitures are not to be found unless the intent is clear or no other interpretation is reasonably possible. Several things could make the intent clear: explicit language, of course, or past practice ratified by re-adoption of general language. The context might also give such an indication. It is so important to most parties that the grievance and arbitration process operate promptly and efficiently, that it is usually assumed that deadlines for filing a grievance or demanding arbitration are meant to be strictly followed. Other steps of the process are not so crucial to efficient handling of grievances and are often held not to work forfeitures. If a union has taken a grievance through the four specified steps of the grievance procedure and timely demanded arbitration, for example, a day's delay in appointing its own member of the arbitration panel will probably not cause it to lose the right to arbitration unless the contract so states.

9. *Harsh, Absurd or Nonsensical Results Should be Avoided if Another Interpretation Would Lead to Just and Reasonable Results*

The parties may occasionally provide for harsh penalties in a contract. A serious absentee problem might lead to a contract clause providing discharge for a first offense or, more likely, to a clause prohibiting the arbitrator from modifying a penalty imposed by the employer if the employee was in fact guilty of an offense. Such clear intentions must be followed, but in their absence it is reasonable to assume that the parties did not expect their agreement to be unduly harsh. It is even less likely that they intended absurd or nonsensical results.

Thus when one possible interpretation would lead to harshness or absurdity, and another to justice and rationality, the latter is to be preferred. This does not mean the arbitrator may amend any agreement to make it more just or reasonable; it simply provides guidance for exercising a choice when the agreement itself admits of several possibilities.

G. THE ARBITRATION AWARD AND OPINION

1. *Form*

The award issued by the arbitrator need not be in any particular form to be legally binding,

[171]

unless the contract, submission agreement or state arbitration statute contains some restriction. Again with the same qualification, it need not even be in writing, although the Voluntary Labor Arbitration Rules of the AAA specify written awards (Appendix 2, Rule 38) and as a matter of practice arbitrators always provide a written decision unless requested by the parties not to do so.

2. *Time Limitations*

Similarly there is in most jurisdictions no legal requirement that the award be issued within a certain period. A few state statutes do require awards to be issued promptly, usually within 30 to 60 days of the hearing, but it is doubtful whether such limitations have any legal effect in labor arbitration cases. A party seeking enforcement of a late award would rely on federal arbitration law developed under Section 301, and to date no federal court has held that state time limits have been incorporated in that law. At least one has held just the opposite, that a state limitation may not be used to frustrate an otherwise fair arbitration. *West Rock Lodge No. 2120, IAM v. Geometric Tool Co.*, 406 F.2d 284 (2d Cir. 1968). It is certainly conceivable that in a case of extreme delay with resulting harm to a party a federal court could apply a version of the equitable doctrine of laches, but even that is unlikely unless the other party is responsible for the delay. The parties may set their own limitations in the contract or submission agreement and the arbitrator would have no authority beyond those limits, but even in the interest of speed such provisions may be unwise. An unexpected illness or other good cause might delay the award by a few days and the losing party would simply have an excuse for not abiding by the award when it did come in. The result would either be a resort to litigation or economic weapons or needless repetition of the arbitration process.

This is not to minimize the importance of prompt decisions. To the contrary, if arbitration is to be more desirable than other forms of dispute resolution it must provide quick decisions, and accordingly the AAA Rules require that the arbitrator render his award "not later than 30 days from the date of closing the hearings" unless otherwise agreed by the parties or specified by law (Appendix 2, Rule 37). Under FMCS regulations, arbitrators are "encouraged" to render awards within 60 days under the threat of harm to their "continuing relationship with the FMCS roster." (Appendix 4, Section 1404.15 (a)). Notwithstanding these rules, delayed awards are a regrettable fact of life, not at all uncommon in this business.

3. Arbitration Panels

When the arbitration is conducted before a panel of arbitrators, a majority vote is usually required for a valid award (Appendix 2, Rule 38). While in many cases this will make good sense, in some cases it may prevent a decision. The neutral arbitrator may desire to render an award falling between the polar positions of the parties but may be unable to convince either side to budge. This would either prevent the arbitrator from making any award, thus forcing the parties to use economic weapons and vitiating the value of the arbitration agreement, or force the arbitrator to move to one pole or the other (and thus at once render a decision he does not favor and further outrage the losing party). An arbitrator might believe that a certain employee offense was reprehensible but not sufficient cause for discharge and thus desire to order reinstatement without back pay. Unless one or the other of the parties is willing to compromise on its initial position, the arbitrator will be unable to obtain a majority vote for his proposed award. To prevent such deadlocks, some agreements have abandoned the tripartite approach in favor of the single arbitrator, and others now provide that if no majority can be obtained the neutral is authorized to issue a binding award or his own.

4. *Content*

Whatever form the award is in, it should resolve all major questions raised. That much is necessary to convince the NLRB to defer under its *Spielberg* policy and to enable a court to enforce the award under *Enterprise Wheel*. More immediately, an award that fails to resolve the major issues will only prolong the dispute between the parties.

The award will not be void simply because it fails to cross some of the T's, however. If the arbitrator awards back pay to certain suspended employees without specifying the exact amounts due to them, the computation is usually left to the parties, although the arbitrator may attempt to retain jurisdiction to resolve disputes over the exact amount due. Or again, if all employees who worked on a certain holiday are found to be entitled to premium pay, the parties may reasonably be expected to fill in the names of those who worked that day. But if, on the other hand, an arbitrator decided that some employees deserve a raise because of added duties but does not tell how much of a raise is appropriate, his award lacks an essential element and may therefore be invalid.

5. *The Opinion*

A supporting opinion may not be required as a matter of law, but the reasons for such opinions are so strong that the Code of Professional Responsibility for Arbitrators of Labor-Management Disputes requires the arbitrator to comply with the expectations of the parties in this regard if they have been communicated to him prior to his acceptance of appointment (Appendix 5, paragraph 121). The practice is so widespread that opinions are routinely expected except in experimental contexts where the parties are willing to trade off the benefits of a reasoned opinion for speed or economy.

What are the benefits to the parties? First, the opinion states the reasons for the award and by doing so demonstrates that the award was in fact a reasoned one. This in turn contributes to the willingness of the parties to accept the award and abide by it. Second, a written opinion provides guidance to the parties in dealing with similar but not identical issues. To the extent that the arbitrator succeeds in providing such guidance in a persuasive manner, he may save the parties from needless future grievances and arbitrations. Third, a reasoned opinion may obviate appeals to other forums. The NLRB will defer to arbitrations awards under its *Spielberg* doctrine only if the arbitrator dealt with the alleged unfair labor practice; in the absence of an opinion it may be difficult to determine whether that condition has been met, and a dissatisfied party would be more optimistic about obtaining a different ruling from the Board. Similarly a court would be less likely to overturn an award backed by a careful opinion, and failure to provide such an opinion might encourage appeals to courts by losing parties.

A cynic could suggest several distinct reasons why an arbitrator would want to write an opinion. Arbitrators are normally paid by the day and writing an opinion will therefore justify a larger fee. Moreover, experienced arbitrators are more likely to be selected by parties than inexperienced arbitrators and one of the main indications of experience is the number of opinions published in the reporting services. An arbitrator might also want to impress other arbitrators, and one way to do this is to provide them the opportunity to read his well-reasoned decisions.

For all of these reasons, formal opinions are generally expected and provided.

6. Termination of the Arbitrator's Authority

The arbitrator can only render a binding award during the time he has jurisdiction. That jurisdiction can be terminated in a number of ways:

(a) *By the Withdrawal of One of the Parties.* Under common law rules an agreement to arbitrate was purely executory and could be terminated by either party up until the time the arbitrator's award was rendered. Such a termination might constitute a breach of contract, but the breach was not specifically enforceable and dam-

[*177*]

ages, being difficult if not impossible to ascertain, were likely to be nominal. After *Lincoln Mills*, it would seem that an attempted withdrawal would be ineffective unless authorized by the contract.

(b) *By Expiration of Time Limits.* Time limitations established in the collective bargaining agreement, the submission agreement or in a separate understanding would be valid if inadvisable, and the arbitrator's authority would expire automatically if those limits were ignored.

(c) *By Rendition of a Final Award.* Under the doctrine of *functus officio* an arbitrator's power ceases when he has completed the task for which he was selected—that is, when he renders a final award. After that action he could not, under common law, reopen the hearing or modify his award without a new grant of authority. Many arbitrators routinely "retain jurisdiction" for 30 to 60 days after a decision is rendered in case the parties have difficulty applying the award. This would have been of dubious effect in pre-Section 301 days, but probably would be enforced today.

(d) *By Operation of Law.* State statutes and common law occasionally provide a few automatic terminations. The most obvious of these is the death or disability of the arbitrator; less obvious (and perhaps irrelevant in most cases today because of the continuing nature of corporate and labor organizations) is the death or disability of one of the parties.

7. Interpretation, Modification or Correction of the Award by the Arbitrator

As mentioned above, at common law the arbitrator's power expired once he rendered a final award and he had no legal authority thereafter to interpret, modify or correct that award. Much of that common law rule remains in effect today. The Code of Professional Responsibility for Arbitrators of Labor-Management Disputes, revised in 1974, states that "No clarification or interpretation of an award is permissible without the consent of both parties" (Appendix 5, paragraph 130) and modifications could stand in no stronger position. If both parties consent, the arbitrator is given a new grant of authority.

There are good policy reasons behind this rule, but there is at least one good argument against it: it forces litigation to correct even the most obvious mistakes or to obtain the simplest of clarifications if one party is obstinate. As a result, some cracks in the doctrine have begun to appear. A few federal courts have ordered cases returned to the arbitrator for clarification in actions to enforce or vacate awards rather than revise the award themselves or force the parties to start over again. The proposed Uniform Arbitration Act explicitly allows arbitrators to modify or correct an award on the application of a single party or on submission by a court if there was "an evident miscalculation of figures or an evident mistake in the description of any person, thing or property referred to in the award" or if the award "is imperfect in a matter of form, not affecting the merits of the controversy." (Appendix 7, Sections 9 and 11.) A few state statutes have similar provisions. Note, however, that in no case does the arbitrator have any power to revise his decision as to the merits of the case. Any questions on that score must either be jointly submitted under a new grant of authority or must be raised before a court in an action to enforce or vacate the arbitrator's award.

8. *Actions to Enforce or Vacate an Arbitrator's Award*

The general principles of judicial review, as established in *Enterprise Wheel* and subsequent cases, have been discussed at length above and will not be repeated here. A few practical aspects of the review process bear mention at this point, however.

First, it should be noted that actions to enforce or vacate an arbitration award are exceedingly rare in labor cases because the parties generally wish to avoid formal legal proceedings and because of the evident futility of challenging an arbitrator's award after the *Steelworkers Trilogy*.

Second, a party that is truly dissatisfied with an award and believes that the award would not be upheld by a court has several options. Which option he takes will depend on the strategy appropriate to the facts of the case. He can take the offensive and bring an action in equity to vacate the award. He may refuse to comply with the award and prepare to defend an action at law for money damages or an action in equity for specific enforcement. There is also a possibility that he may simply refuse to comply with the award and will win by default if the other party takes no further legal action. It should hardly be necessary to add that actions of this sort do not lead to very good labor relations.

Once a court issues an order enforcing an award, disobedience of that order is almost unheard of. In theory the violator would be guilty of civil or criminal contempt of court and could be punished accordingly. In one noteworthy case, a court of appeals affirmed a fine of $100,000 per day levied by a district court against a union in such a situation. *Philadelphia Marine Trade Ass'n v. ILA, Local 1291,* 368 F.2d 932 (3d Cir. 1966), rev'd on other grounds 389 U.S. 64 (1967).

It is not yet clear whether the prevailing party in an action to enforce or vacate an award is entitled to costs and attorneys fees. Most courts have refused to grant such payments because federal law does not specifically provide for them, but at least one circuit court has disagreed. *International Union of District 50, UMW v. Bowman Trans., Inc.,* 421 F.2d 934 (5th Cir. 1970).

VI

TOPICS OF CURRENT CONCERN IN LABOR ARBITRATION

A. REMEDIES

1. In General

The broad power the Supreme Court deemed arbitrators to have extends to remedies as well as to interpretation. As Justice Douglas put it in *Enterprise Wheel,*

> When an arbitrator is commissioned to interpret and apply the collective bargaining agreement, he is to bring his informed judgment to bear in order to reach a fair solution of a problem. This is especially true when it comes to formulating remedies. There the need is for flexibility in meeting a wide variety of situations. The draftsmen may never have thought of what specific remedy should be awarded to meet a particular contingency.

Similarly, the Uniform Arbitration Act states that "the fact that the relief was such that it could not or would not be granted by a court of law or equity is not ground for vacating or refusing to confirm the award." (Appendix 7, Section 12(a) (5)).

Arbitrators have not been hesitant to exercise this power to the fullest. In one notable case the arbitrator, after finding that the employer breached the contract in transferring work, ordered it at great expense to reverse the earlier decision, return the work and the equipment used to perform it from Arkansas and Colorado to St. Louis, recall laid off employees and reinstate them with full back pay—and the order was enforced in full by the federal courts. *Selb Mfg. Co. v. I.A.M. District No. 9*, 305 F.2d 177 (8th Cir. 1962).

Once again it should be emphasized that the arbitrator draws his power from the contract. If the parties fear that an arbitrator might order a remedy they regard as inappropriate they can prevent such an occurrence in any of a number of ways. Some contracts simply place certain types of remedies off limits; others specify the remedy to be applied in the event of a certain breach; and still others limit the arbitrator's role to a determination of whether there has in fact been a breach, leaving the selection of a remedy to the parties themselves.

2. Discharge Cases

If an arbitrator finds that an employee was wrongly discharged, the typical remedy is reinstatement with full seniority and back pay. This is not always the case, however. Because an arbitrator will examine the alleged misdeeds, the degree of the penalty imposed and the procedure followed, it is quite common for him to seek some middle ground between the positions of the parties.

If an employee did in fact commit the charged offense but the arbitrator believes that discharge was too harsh a penalty, he might order conditional reinstatement (thus creating a form of probationary employment) or reinstatement with reduced or no back pay. He might feel, for example, that repeated tardiness would justify only a week's suspension and order reinstatement with back pay for the time off work less one week. Or if the union unjustifiably delayed in bringing the case to arbitration, he might order reinstatement less pay for the length of the delay.

Arbitrators will generally insist on even-handed administration of discipline—that is, that like penalties be imposed for like offenses. At the same time they recognize that there are many valid reasons for distinguishing between employees. If a large number of employees participate in a wildcat strike, for example, discharge of all might not be practical and most arbitrators would therefore uphold discharge of the leaders of the strike but not others, or of participating union officials (who are presumed to know the contract and be specially charged with obeying it) but not others. All that must be shown is that the basis of selection is fair and sensible.

3. *Monetary Awards in Non-Discharge Cases*

Many other sorts of breaches can be best redressed by monetary awards. In general, however, there must be a showing of actual loss and the amount awarded must not exceed the amount necessary to compensate the wronged party. More than that would be punitive, and with rare exceptions discussed below, punitive damages are inappropriate in labor arbitration. For the same reason and with the same exceptions, no damages should be awarded when the harm, if any, is too speculative to calculate.

It may sometimes be necessary to make rough approximations of the amount of damage, and so long as the arbitrator does so in good faith his award is unlikely to be overturned. In *Local 369, Bakery and Confectionary Workers v. Cotton Baking Co.*, 514 F.2d 1235 (5th Cir. 1975), cert. denied 423 U.S. 1055 (1976), the employer was found to have failed to use bargaining unit employees for certain bargaining unit work. It could not be shown that any individual lost any wages as a result of the breach, but it was clear that the bargaining unit as a whole had suffered. Accordingly the arbitrator ordered monetary damages to the union in the amount of one year's wages for the job in question, and his award was upheld by the Court of Appeals.

Monetary damages have also been awarded **against** unions, usually for breach of a no-strike

[*185*]

agreement. This should not be surprising, for such agreements would quickly become a nullity if the harm due to breaches could not be compensated. Usually arbitrators will insist on some evidence of union authorization or approval of a strike, but in a few cases they have held that the union may properly be charged solely because it did not try to stop the strike, apparently on the theory that as representative of the employees the union has the obligation to lead the employees in the proper direction and may not simply abdicate that responsibility.

Awards against unions require a contract permitting an employer to file a grievance. Many contracts lack such a provision, and damages for union breaches could then come only from a court.

4. Calculation of the Amount of Damages

In some cases there may be difficulty determining how much harm was suffered by the grievant. The arbitrator need not calculate the exact amount due, so long as he provides some formula the parties can apply. Usually a general order to reinstate a discharged employee "with full back pay" will suffice, for the parties can calculate the wage rate times the number of lost hours.

There may be complications, though, and if the parties do not have a good relationship it may be necessary for an arbitrator to resolve a dispute over the exact amount of back pay due. Most arbitrators will subtract alternative earnings from the back pay award on the ground that the award should only compensate for actual loss. Following a general rule of contract law, many arbitrators would also subtract the earnings the employee could have had, had he sought work with due diligence. There is no simple rule about unemployment compensation. Some arbitrators ignore it entirely, while others (noting that it is the employer, not the employee, who pays for unemployment compensation) will deduct it from the amount of back pay due. The proper decision on unemployment compensation will consider whether recoupment by the state is required under state law; if so, there is less reason for the arbitrator to deduct it from his award.

In all cases the arbitrator should ascertain the amount of harm due to the breach and award only that amount. Thus if the employer's judgment that an employee was too ill to work was initially wrong but later was accurate, damages are appropriate only for the time the employer was wrong.

The problems of calculation are much greater when the employer seeks damages from the union, for there is typically no simple hourly rate to be applied. Among the standards applied in wrongful strike situations are (1) the average daily "overhead cost," or expenses incident to maintenance of the plant; (2) overhead cost plus the amount of overtime pay needed to catch up on lost production; (3) fair rental value of idle machinery; and (4) loss of profits.

Interest on monetary damages has been awarded by a few arbitrators, but generally interest is not a customary item and is seldom even requested by the grievant. It is almost unheard of where the dispute involves only a good faith disagreement about the meaning of the contract. Some of those who have awarded interest have explained their decision in terms of the bad faith or arbitrariness of the contract breaches at issue—in other words, the interest award is levied as a form of punitive damages. Those who do not award interest sometimes note that the monetary award itself is generous in discharge cases in that the employee is being paid for a period in which he performed no work.

5. *Punitive Damages*

Arbitrators who are asked to award punitive damages must confront a dilemma of arbitration theory. Punishment and retribution are concepts foreign to the purpose of arbitration, the amicable settlement of disputes, yet in many cases punitive damages are the only means the arbitrator has to provide an incentive for obeying the contract or to shift the burden of proving actual harm from the innocent party to the guilty one.

The courts have been similarly ambivalent. One early, much criticized decision refused to enforce an award of punitive damages because they would not be appropriate in a normal breach of contract suit. *Publishers Ass'n of New York City v. Newspaper and Mail Deliverers' Union of New York and Vicinity,* 280 App.Div. 500, 114 N. Y.S.2d 401 (1952). More recent cases have simply interpreted Section 301 to be remedial, not punitive, *e. g., United Shoe Workers Local 127 v. Brooks Mfg., Co.,* 298 F.2d 277 (3d Cir. 1962).

Nevertheless some arbitrators have awarded punitive damages in cases of willful violations, where the wrong was inflicted maliciously, or where it is impossible to determine the actual damage caused by a serious breach. And in a few cases federal courts have enforced such awards, *e. g., Local 416 Sheetmetal Workers International Ass'n v. Helgesteel Corp.,* 335 F.Supp. 812 (W.D., Wis.1971) rev'd on other grounds 507 F.2d 1053 (7th Cir. 1974) (relying on broad arbitral power discussed in the *Trilogy*).

In many cases the difference between true compensatory relief and a punitive award may be slender indeed. This is especially true when there has been some harm but the amount is intangible. A rough estimate might be labeled compensatory when it is in reality only an amount selected to punish the wrongdoer.

6. *"Injunctive" or "Cease-and-Desist" Relief*

In such cases of intangible harm, and in many other types of cases as well, the arbitrator frequently will order the wrongdoer to cease breaching the contract. Such orders are not properly termed injunctions because they do not have the force of law behind them. In the early days of arbitration it was believed that courts might be prohibited by federal or state anti-injunction acts from enforcing such awards by their own injunctions. In light of *Boys Markets* that fear seems baseless. So long as the arbitrator's award draws its essence from the collective bargaining agreement, it is valid and can be enforced by an appropriate court.

7. *Rights Without Remedies*

There are a number of situations in which an arbitrator is likely to find that there has been a breach of the agreement but that no remedy should be issued. The most common of these is where the breach is *de minimis*, as where a supervisor performs a few minutes of work that should be assigned to a bargaining unit member. There is good reason to feel that the *de minimis* doctrine ought to be used in arbitration only to determine the amount of damages and not as a reason for dismissing the grievance. While the law does not concern itself about trifles, collective bargaining (and, perforce, labor arbitration) does. A minor event may involve a principle of some magnitude (preserving a rigid seniority system or guaranteeing that work will be kept in the bargaining unit, for example). And there is always the therapeutic value of arbitration, a value that would disappear in any case dismissed as trifling.

Other cases in which no remedy would be awarded include those where the breach is not *de minimis* but the harm resulting therefrom is not measurable (*e. g.*, where a requirement that the employer give notice to the union before taking certain action is ignored) or where there is no accurate information as to which employee is entitled to damages (*e. g.*, where at some time during a shift the employer should have called in another employee, but it is uncertain which of many would have been called or available). Even in these cases the arbitrator would be better advised to issue some remedy such as a cease-and-desist order rather than simply to dismiss the grievance. In a few cases parties ask only for a declaration of rights, and a monetary award would not be appropriate in such a case.

B. THE EFFECT OF CONTRACT TERMINATION

Difficult questions are presented by demands for arbitration following termination of the contract containing the arbitration clause. (It seems to be clear that termination does not affect the arbitrability of a dispute for which arbitration was requested before termination, but expiration of the contract might limit the remedies available.) Even though the Supreme Court has dealt with such cases several times, most of the decisions involved a complicating factor that is best discussed separately, the presence of a successor employer, and thus do not directly resolve some fundamental issues. At stake is a clash between basic principles of contract law, which refuse to hold a party to the terms of an agreement after its expiration, and the fundamental policy of federal labor law favoring arbitration.

The termination problem can occur in three situations: (1) where the grievance sought to be arbitrated arose before the contract expired, but arbitration would take place after termination; (2) where the grievance arose after termination but is based on a right that arguably accrued or "vested" prior to termination; and (3) where the grievance arose after termination and depends on the continuance of rights of a non-accruing type established in the terminated contract.

The first situation was dealt with by the Supreme Court in *John Wiley & Sons, Inc. v. Livingston,* 376 U.S. 543 (1964). A unionized employer, Interscience Publishers, Inc., merged with the larger, nonunion firm of John Wiley & Sons. The union sought arbitration of several grievances, some of which sought continuation of the contract beyond the termination date. Wiley refused but on appeal the Court ordered arbitration on all the grievances. In very broad dicta the court cited national labor policy as requiring some balance of protection for employees threatened by a sudden change in the employment relationship, and said that industrial strife would be avoided if employees' claims continued to be resolved by arbitration rather than by the relative strength of the parties. The Court recognized that expiration of the contract might affect some of the claims, but felt that that consideration went to the merits and should be weighed by the arbitrator rather than the courts. Interestingly, in one subsequent arbitration case, the arbitrator did weigh that factor, holding that the seniority provision was extinguished by the termination of the contract containing it. *Interscience Encyclopedia Inc.*, 55 LA 210 (B. Roberts, 1970).

The Supreme Court recently dealt with the second situation in *Nolde Bros. v. Local No. 358, Bakery & Confectionery Workers Union*, 430 U.S. 243 (1977). The employer closed the plant after the contract terminated, but the union sought arbitration of its demand for severance pay, claiming that the right to it accrued during the term of the contract. The Supreme Court noted that nothing in the contract actually **prohibited** arbitration of the claim and ordered the parties to go to arbitration. In doing so the Court cited the federal policy favoring arbitration and its *Wiley* decision, but relied heavily on the fact that the union's claim was based on an obligation "arguably created by the expired agreement."

The third situation has not been directly addressed by the Supreme Court. Some unions have argued that contractual rights such as protection from discharge except for just cause and a prohibition on lockouts continue even beyond the expiration of the contract. Most courts to consider the issue have rejected that argument, pointing out that it would mean that an employer who once agreed to submit its managerial actions to arbitration did so for all time. *See, e. g., Procter & Gamble Independent Union of Port Ivory, N. Y. v. Procter & Gamble Mfg. Co.*, 312 F.2d 181 (2d Cir. 1962), cert. denied 374 U.S. 830 (1973); *Local 998, U.A.W. v. B & T Metals*, 315 F.2d 432 (6th Cir. 1963).

C. SUCCESSORSHIP

The Supreme Court has decided three major cases bearing upon the effect of an arbitration agreement on a successor employer. In *John Wiley & Sons*, an action under Section 301, the Court held that a successor employer could be required to arbitrate pursuant to the predecessor's collective bargaining agreement, at least in situations where there is "substantial continuity in the business enterprise before and after a change." In *NLRB v. Burns International Security Services, Inc.*, 406 U.S. 272 (1972), an unfair labor practice case, the court held that a successor employer was obliged to bargain with the union representing his predecessor's employees if those employees constitute a majority of the new work force. More importantly for the current topic, it held that the successor was not obliged to apply the terms of the predecessor's contract with that union. Finally, in *Howard Johnson Co. v. Detroit Local Joint Executive Board*, 417 U.S. 249 (1974), another Section 301 action, it held that a successor need not arbitrate pursuant to the predecessor's contract where there is no "substantial continuity of identity in the business enterprise" (only a small percentage of the new work force in that case had been in the previous bargaining unit).

Clearly these cases do not mesh neatly. In particular, the holding in *Burns* that a successor is not bound by the predecessor's contract seems to be at odds both with the holding of *Wiley* (that the successor is bound by a part—the arbitration clause—of the predecessor's contract) and with *Wiley's* implication that the arbitrator could find the successor bound by all of the terms of the contract. It is possible to distinguish the two cases (one was a merger, the other a sale; one was brought in court under Sec. 301, the other before the NLRB) but the distinctions are not persuasive and the Supreme Court expressly rejected the latter distinction in *Howard Johnson*. It is likely that there will be further attempts by the Court to settle successorship problems, but until then a few rules can be formulated.

First, a successor employer is likely to be required to arbitrate pursuant to an agreement in the predecessor's contract where there is substantial continuity of the business enterprise.

Second, where substantial continuity is lacking —where, for example, new employees form a majority or the old employees are dispersed throughout the new employer's operations—the successor is under no obligation to arbitrate under the predecessor's agreement.

Third, where the successor does arbitrate, the arbitrator may hold it bound by the substantive terms of the agreement and the courts may enforce such a holding.

The last point deserves some explanation. After the Court's decision in *John Wiley & Sons*, there was an arbitration that raised the question of the effect of the contract terms on the new employer. The arbitrator held that the successor was bound by that agreement until its expiration or until a change of conditions occurred that altered or abolished the separate identity of the old bargaining unit, whichever came first. *Intersci-*

ence Encyclopedia, Inc., 55 LA 210 (B. Roberts, 1970). Another arbitrator reached a similar conclusion in *United States Gypsum Co.*, 56 LA 363 (Valtin, 1971) and his award was enforced *sub nom. United Steelworkers v. United States Gypsum Co.*, 492 F.2d 713 (5th Cir. 1974).

VII

APPLICATION OF ARBITRATION TO NEW SITUATIONS

A. THE PUBLIC SECTOR

1. The Federal Government

Collective bargaining is a relatively recent development in the federal government, and arbitration as a means of dispute settlement is just as new. The first major step toward labor arbitration in the federal sector came in 1962, when President Kennedy issued Executive Order 10988. This was immediately hailed as a "Magna Carta" for public employees, but it was but a pale reflection of the private sector collective bargaining system. Among other limitations, the Order allowed only advisory arbitration of contract disputes.

In 1969 President Nixon issued Executive Order 11491, which constituted a major revision of federal labor relations. The new executive order governed federal sector labor relations until 1978, when the Civil Service Reform Act, P.L. 95–454, was adopted. That Act finally established a statutory scheme of labor relations for the federal government.

For instant purposes, the most important part of the new law is Title VII, which is codified at

5 U.S.C.A. Section 7101 *et seq.* For ease of reference, citations herein are to the appropriate sections of the Code.

The new law provides for both interest arbitration and grievance arbitration. In the event of a negotiation impasse, the Federal Services Impasses Panel (FSIP) is directed to consider the matter on request of either party. Alternatively the parties may themselves adopt a procedure for binding arbitration, but only if the procedure is approved by the FSIP. If the FSIP considers the matter itself and is unable to bring about a settlement, it may "take whatever action is necessary and not inconsistent with this chapter to resolve the impasse," and the action taken "shall be binding on such parties during the term of the agreement, unless the parties agree otherwise." 5 U.S.C.A. Section 7119.

The new law is equally insistent on grievance arbitration. It requires that unless the parties agree otherwise all collective bargaining agreements are to establish a system of binding arbitration for the resolution of grievances. There are a few statutory exceptions (*e. g.*, disputes over examination, certification or appointment, or involving retirement or insurance plans), but the clear intention is to make arbitration the normal method of resolving disputes. 5 U.S.C.A. Section 7121.

A party dissatisfied with an arbitration award may file an exception with the Federal Labor Relations Authority which is authorized to take action if it finds that the award is contrary to any law, rule or regulation or is deficient "on other grounds similar to those applied by Federal courts in private sector labor-management relations." If no exception is filed, the award becomes final and binding after 30 days. 5 U.S.C.A. Section 7122.

Arbitration agreements have become widespread in the federal government. By one recent count, 90% of the government's collective bargaining agreements contained provisions for arbitration of at least some disputes. There has been a good deal of criticism, however, particularly from unions. One major complaint is the limited subject matter. Because many of the most important terms of employment are controlled by statute rather than contract (among them wages, hours, overtime pay, holidays, vacations, pensions and insurance) disputes on those topics are not arbitrable. Another problem is that arbitration awards requiring expenditure of funds have been in effect appealable to the Comptroller General. In the past this was frequently done, because an employee who spends government funds without authorization could be personally liable. More importantly, the Comptroller, whose primary concern is protection of the Treasury rather than promotion of the collective bargaining system, frequently used his power to reverse the arbitrator. This happens less frequently today, but is still a cause of concern. It is not yet clear whether the Civil Service Reform Act affects the comptroller's power in this regard, but by providing a statutory basis for arbitral awards the new law should discourage such appeals. A third difficulty is that, except for claimed violations of constitutional rights, judicial review of arbitration awards is not easily available. Courts asked to intervene in these cases have usually taken the position that they have no power to resolve disputes that are purely within the executive branch.

2. *State and Local Governments*

Local governments vary widely in their use of labor arbitration. Some states still prohibit collective bargaining with public employees. Others permit bargaining but do not regard negotiated agreements as binding; in such a situation either party could refuse to proceed with an arbitration or to abide by an award. In still other states, courts have held contractual arbitration agreements, even when authorized by statute, unconstitutional as a prohibited delegation of governmental power to a private individual.

Notwithstanding these exceptions, it is safe to say that in most states public sector labor arbitration is both legal and common. Moreover, some states have led the way in development of new forms of arbitration, in particular compulsory, expedited, "final-offer" and interest arbitration, about which more will be said below.

It is impossible to describe completely all of the varieties of arbitration practiced by state and local governments, and it would probably be useless to try because of the rapidity of changes in this area. A few general comments are all that will be offered here.

First, with regard to grievance arbitration, it would seem that most arbitration agreements and most awards rendered pursuant to them are similar to those found in the private sector. The most important exceptions to the rule are the rather more frequent use in the public sector of advisory arbitration and the greater care with which the parties limit the scope of arbitration (presumably to avoid the sort of court rulings mentioned above).

Second, it seems that state courts are less reluctant to grant judicial review of public sector arbitration awards than of private sector awards. Perhaps the state courts feel that their role is greater when federal law and policy are not involved.

Third, the states and localities frequently mandate arbitration as an alternative to strikes. Compulsory arbitration is virtually unknown in the private sector—even the national emergency procedures set forth in the Taft-Hartley Act only require mediation.

Fourth, interest arbitration—that is, arbitration of disputes over the terms to be included in a collective bargaining agreement, as opposed to disputes concerning the interpretation or application of contract terms—is not yet common in the public sector, but it does take place more often in local government than elsewhere. Of the major industries, only steel has adopted interest arbitration; of the major divisions of the federal government, only the postal service uses it, although this will change under the Civil Service Reform Act of 1978. By way of contrast, several states have adopted interest arbitration procedures in statute or contract, chiefly for employees charged with protecting public safety.

B. HIGHER EDUCATION

Arbitration provisions covering colleges and universities do not differ markedly from those in other types of employment situations except in their exclusions. Tenure, retention and promotion disputes constitute the bulk of faculty grievances but many contracts exclude questions of "academic judgment" from arbitration. Definition of that term varies, but it usually includes the criteria under which personnel decisions are made and the ways in which the criteria are applied. Thus an arbitrator could decide whether contractual procedures (or institutional rules incorporated in the contract) were followed, and in some cases may decide whether academic judgment was used at all, but frequently will be prohibited from second-guessing the evaluation of teaching or research made by the relevant committee or administrator.

Where the arbitrator is allowed to act in faculty personnel cases, he will be faced with a serious problem of determining the standards to apply. A few contracts spell out the requirements for retention, promotion and so on, but more are either so general as to be of little help or are completely silent. University policy and past practice can flesh out such contracts, but even these are seldom conclusive.

A number of arbitrators have resolved the problem by applying a standard of reasonableness, similar to that a reviewing court would apply to an administrative agency decision. In essence, this approach upholds the university management once it states a *prima facie* case for its decision unless the grievant can show that the decision was arbitrary, capricious, illegal or otherwise violated the contract. Needless to say, it is hard to meet such a burden of proof. The possible unfairness of this approach is sometimes modified by the heavy presumption given to peer judgments by arbitrators familiar with academic governance. To put it more clearly, such arbitrators require an institution of higher education to show good cause why a favorable peer judgment of the candidate's qualifications was not accepted.

C. ATHLETICS

Collective bargaining was not a major force in professional sports until relatively recent times. As a result, arbitration too is relatively new in this area.

Arbitration systems vary from sport to sport, but almost all of the systems differ from those in other industries in two important respects: first, salary disputes are far more likely to be resolved by an arbitrator; and second, more subjects are exempted from arbitration.

Labor relations in major league baseball are more advanced than in other sports, but the experience there is instructive. Until the 1960's, the club owners had almost total unilateral control of the terms and conditions of employment. When the players' union negotiated its first contract in the 1960's, one of its key demands was a system of impartial arbitration of grievances. It was unable to achieve this objective and was forced to settle instead for a grievance system that ended with arbitration before the commissioner of baseball, who was selected and paid by the same club owners with whom the union was in dispute. One players' representative was fond of describing this system as "partial arbitration," a *double entendre* of some accuracy.

Eventually the club owners chose as their new commissioner Bowie Kuhn, an attorney who had represented the owners in the 1968 negotiations. Clearly Kuhn could not claim to be an objective interpretor of the contract he helped to draft, and the parties therefore selected baseball's first impartial arbitrator to handle the remaining cases under that contract. In the 1970 contract the parties formally adopted impartial arbitration (in the form of a tripartite panel) for disputes, although the commissioner retained the last word on matters involving the integrity of the game.

Unions of athletes have generally refrained from negotiating about salaries, preferring to leave the precise amount above a stated minimum to the agreement of the player and the club. Unresolved salary disputes seriously impair a team's performance, however, and it was therefore imperative to baseball players and owners alike to find a method to settle such disputes promptly. The parties have settled on an approach called "high-low" arbitration which is a variant form of the "final offer" interest arbitration discussed below.

Under the "high-low" system, the player and the team submit their last salary offers to an arbitra-

tor who must choose one or the other of them—
the high or the low figure. No other issues are involved in the arbitration, and no opinion is rendered. According to the report of one arbitrator
who has served in baseball salary disputes, the
"high-low" system has resulted in a battle of statistics. The arbitrator is showered with information about batting averages, runs batted in, earned
run averages, and so on. In the end, gut reaction
inevitably plays a large role. Other reports suggest that the risk factor causes the parties to narrow their differences before proceeding to arbitration, but it does not appear to keep them from
arbitration altogether.

Baseball arbitrations have dealt with broader
issues as well, among them well-publicized disputes over the "reserve" system limiting the player's ability to contract with the team of his choice,
the cancellation of individual player contracts, and
the renewal or option year before a player can become a "free agent" for negotiating purposes.

Arbitration provisions are narrower in other
sports. In professional football almost all disputes
are decided by the Commissioner. Basketball
and hockey provisions are not so restricted, but
neither are they as broad as baseball's.

D. OCCUPATIONAL SAFETY AND HEALTH

Many collective bargaining agreements, particularly those covering hazardous occupations, have long contained provisions relating to occupational safety and health. Typically these provisions authorize or require the employer to take reasonable steps to protect bargaining unit employees. Frequently the contract establishes a joint safety committee, and occasionally it will provide for mutual determination of safety rules and practices.

Concern in recent years about safety and health on the job has led to a significant increase in arbitration awards dealing with this topic. The two major issues in these arbitrations are employer actions to promote safety or health that are challenged on contractual grounds, and discipline of employees who refuse to obey an order because they believe it would endanger themselves or others.

Even where the contract is silent on the point, arbitrators almost uniformly hold that an employer may impose and enforce reasonable safety rules. Almost as uniformly, they hold that employers have the right and responsibility to take immediate action to eliminate a danger. For example, if an employee has a physical or mental disability that constitutes a threat to himself or others, the employer may transfer or suspend him. Similarly, even without express contractual authorization an employer may require an employee on medical leave to provide evidence that he has recovered before allowing him to return to work. Whatever rules are adopted or actions taken must meet the usual criteria, of course: they must bear a clear relationship to their ostensible purpose, must be reasonable in content and fairly applied, and in the case of work rules, must be adequately communicated to the affected employees.

There is more division on the second issue, discipline of employees who refuse assignments they believe to be dangerous. The usual "obey now, grieve later" rule is applicable in this context as well as others, but most arbitrators recognize a narrow implied exception to the rule for disobedience prompted by a serious imminent risk to health or safety. Certain risks are inherent in particular jobs, and these do not come within the exception. A roofer may not refuse a normal roofing assignment because he has developed a fear of heights, nor can a utility lineman refuse to climb a normal pole because of fear of a shock. Moreover, the exception is limited to the employees within the zone of danger; others who are not involved have no license to strike over the disputed assignment.

When such a refusal does occur, an arbitrator may be forced to find a formula that will distinguish between justified and unjustified fears. Their answers have ranged from the purely subjective or "good faith" standard to the purely objective or "real and imminent danger" test. Between these is a compromise approach, requiring that the employee's fear be both in good faith and a reasonable response to the actual circumstances.

The compromise approach is attractive, but one recent study concluded that the vast majority of arbitrators choose the purely objective test. This may stem from the Supreme Court's decision in *Gateway Coal v. United Mine Workers,* 414 U.S. 368 (1974). The union in that case struck to enforce its demand that the employer suspend two foremen who allegedly falsified measurements of air flow in a mine, a matter of great concern to miners. The Court held that where the parties had agreed to submit grievances to arbitration the union could not strike in disregard of that agreement even over safety questions. Section 502 of the Labor-Management Relations Act, which provides that

> . . . the quitting of labor by an employee or employees in good faith because of abnormally dangerous conditions for work at the place of employment of such employee or employees [shall not] be deemed a strike
>
> . . .

did not protect the union, said the Court. A union

seeking to justify a contractually prohibited strike under Section 502 must present "ascertainable, objective evidence supporting its conclusion that an abnormally dangerous condition for work exists," not simply a generalized doubt about the competence of some supervisors.

The *Gateway Coal* decision did not bind arbitrators, but many of them have taken a cue from it and lean more to the objective than the subjective approach.

VIII

VARIATIONS ON TRADITIONAL LABOR ARBITRATION

One of the greatest strengths of labor arbitration is its flexibility. It has changed over time to meet the needs of particular industries, companies and unions, to address new issues, and to respond to pressures from the public and legislatures. This chapter will survey a few of the most significant variations on the traditional labor arbitration system discussed in the preceding pages.

A. EXPEDITED ARBITRATION

"Expedited arbitration" may be a misnomer. Arbitration from its inception was intended to be "expedited" and expedited arbitration should be the norm rather than the variation. Nevertheless, as arbitration proceedings have become formalized, the time from filing a grievance to receipt of the arbitrator's award has lengthened considerably, and some parties have sought ways to speed things up. Particular expedited arbitration systems vary, but they have in common three ways to minimize delays: (a) some form of automatic selection of the arbitrator; (b) a very short period during which the arbitration must take place; and (c) a requirement that the award be made promptly after the close of the hearing, usually within a week.

The steel industry was the first major part of the economy to adopt an expedited arbitration system. Both management and labor came to realize that a large backlog of grievances was undermining the strength of the grievance and arbitration provisions of their contract. In 1971 a joint study commission recommended, and negotiators for both sides adopted a plan for quick decisions on the simpler sort of grievances, chiefly discipline cases turning on factual questions.

The new plan involved the establishment of a special panel of arbitrators for each plant. The total number of participating arbitrators is about 200, most of them new to this business and thus not as likely to be booked up as more experienced arbitrators would be. Assignments are made from this panel in rotation, so there are no disagreements over selection. If the chosen arbitrator is unable to hear the case within 10 days, the next panel member will be called upon. The arbitrator is expected either to render a bench decision at the close of the hearing or to provide a short decision within 48 hours. Procedures at the hearing are informal, and neither party is to use an attorney. Decisions are nonprecedential, and that fact helped to ease fears that novice arbitrators would make serious mistakes.

Early reports indicate that the new system has worked well. The pattern and quality of decisions does not seem to differ substantially from traditional arbitration, and there have been several indirect benefits: the expedited cases have decreased the regular arbitration case load, and there is a better attitude toward arbitration on the part of those immediately affected, the grievant and his supervisors. Perhaps the best indication of the experiment's success is that the parties adopted it in subsequent collective bargaining agreements, and the steelworkers even incorporated it in their agreements for aluminum and container company workers.

In the early 1970's the postal service was facing the same problems with its arbitration system the steel industry had faced a few years earlier. A serious backlog of grievances caused lengthy delays in obtaining arbitration awards, which in turn led to the loss of evidence and a weakening of confidence in arbitration as a method of dispute resolution. The postal service and the major postal unions adopted an expedited arbitration system for certain types of disciplinary cases in their 1973 national agreement to solve these problems.

The procedure adopted was similar to the steel industry's plan. A panel of some 200 arbitrators was selected from the AAA and FMCS lists. As arbitrations come up, the arbitration agency selects the arbitrator from the appropriate list. Proceedings are informal, and there are no briefs or transcripts. The arbitrator may render a bench award but more often he will issue a brief written award shortly after the hearing. In either case the decision carries no precedential force and may not even be cited in subsequent arbitrations. If the case appears to raise complicated issues or to involve a fundamental principle, either party can remand it to the regular grievance-arbitration process.

As with the steel industry, the postal service and its unions were sufficiently satisfied with expedited arbitration to adopt it in later agreements and even to expand its use. By 1977, the parties began to send many non-discipline cases turning on factual determinations to the expedited process. There has been one major modification of the original plan. Because many issues which seem to be local actually raise issues of regional or national concern, the parties have established a screening committee to decide which cases should receive expedited treatment.

Expedited arbitration is easily available to any parties wishing to use it. The American Arbitration Association has established a set of Expedited Labor Arbitration Rules (Appendix 3) which can be incorporated by reference in collective bargaining agreements, or adopted on a case-by-case basis. These contain the three key elements of an expedited system mentioned earlier: selection of an arbitrator by the agency (Rule 2), prompt scheduling of the hearing (Rule 6) and issuance of the award shortly after the hearing (Rule 19).

B. COMPULSORY ARBITRATION

At first glance compulsory arbitration of negotiation disputes seems to be a simple alternative to strikes and lockouts. Apart from the fact that it simply doesn't work in many cases—unions may still strike if dissatisfied with the arbitration award, and sanctions are seldom applied and less often effective—there are strong theoretical objections to it. Briefly, these are that compulsory arbitration is repugnant to the principle of voluntarism on which our labor relations system is based and that it weakens the incentive of the parties to reach their own agreement.

Nevertheless, compulsory arbitration has been often suggested and has even been adopted in several circumstances. Perhaps the first major attempt to establish a system of compulsory arbitration came with state statutes long before the Wagner Act was passed. The Supreme Court quickly struck these down as an unconstitutional taking of property, *Wolff Packing Co. v. Court of Industrial Relations,* 262 U.S. 522 (1923); *Dorchy v. Kansas,* 264 U.S. 286 (1924).

The next attempt came in 1942 with President Roosevelt's Executive Order 9017, which established the National War Labor Board. Section 3 of that Order provided that once the Board took jurisdiction of a case it should "finally determine the dispute and for this purpose [it] may use mediation, voluntary arbitration or arbitration under the rules established by the Board." Disputes were often assigned to a single hearing officer or to a tripartite panel which submitted a recommended decision to the Board; the Board's decision was final and binding.

The National War Labor Board was not completely without federal precedent, for the Railway Labor Act provided for compulsory arbitration of grievances (as opposed to negotiation disputes) before the National Railroad Adjustment Board, a group of arbitrators selected and paid by the major railroad employers and unions. Twice in recent years Congress has by special legislation commanded arbitration of negotiation disputes concerning firemen on diesel trains and crew size.

After World War II, the initiative in compulsory arbitration shifted back to the states, and several of them adopted laws applicable to public utilities. Like the earlier state statutes, these were struck down by the Supreme Court, *Amalgamated Association of Street, Electric Railway and Motor Coach Employees of America, Division 998 v. Wisconsin Employment Relations Board*, 340 U.S. 383 (1951). This time the basis of the decision was preemption of state action by the National Labor Relations Act.

Since that time compulsory arbitration has often been proposed as a solution to private sector labor disputes affecting the national economy or creating emergencies in particular areas. With the exception of the two railroad statutes mentioned above, Congress has not gone along with these suggestions.

Several states have adopted compulsory arbitration in an area over which unconstitutional taking and preemption arguments have no sway— that is, in disputes involving employees of state and local governments. The federal government has done the same with regard to one group of its own employees, postal workers. Under the Postal Reorganization Act of 1970, unresolved disputes over contract negotiations are presented to an arbitrator empowered to establish contract terms. This provision was first used in 1978 and successfully averted a threatened postal strike. As mentioned above, other federal employees now have a form of compulsory arbitration as a result of the Civil Service Reform Act of 1978.

State compulsory arbitration statutes are usually but not always limited to public safety and fire prevention employee disputes. Most use *ad hoc* impartial arbitrators, frequently on a tripartite board, and most contain some provisions intended to encourage settlement and discourage use of arbitration. Several require mediation efforts and fact-finding procedures (discussed below) as a prelude to arbitration, for example, some give a labor relations agency power to refuse arbitration, and some require that the parties share the cost of arbitration.

Judicial review of compulsory arbitration awards is always available, but sometimes it is limited to constitutional or scope of authority issues. More often, review is available on the same standards applied to administrative actions generally; that is, the awards are to be upheld unless they exceed statutory authorization, are constitutionally infirm, or are arbitrary, capricious or unreasonable. A number of state laws have been struck down as unconstitutional delegations of government power to a private individual, but most courts have upheld statutes where reasonable criteria for the arbitration award are specified or implied.

C. FACT–FINDING AND ADVISORY ARBITRATION

Fact-finding and advisory arbitration are similar methods of bringing impartial expert opinions to bear on collective bargaining disputes without surrendering the right of each party to reject that advice.

VARIATIONS ON ARBITRATION

1. The Private Sector

These processes are seldom used in the private sector, although the Railway Labor Act and the Taft-Hartley Act provide for fact-finding panels in certain cases of unresolved negotiation disputes. These panels have occasionally helped to resolve bargaining impasses, but not so regularly that the process has been widely adopted.

Advisory arbitration has been successfully employed for many years in one field, that of wire service reporting systems. The contracts of the United Telegraph Workers with the Associated Press and the United Press International provide that if negotiations do not result in an agreement, the parties will each appoint a single representative to make a further attempt to reach a settlement. If that fails, the two representatives will select a neutral person to chair a tripartite arbitration panel. The panel holds evidentiary hearings and uses executive sessions and mediation on individual items to produce a settlement. If a settlement is not reached, the panel issues an opinion which must be accepted or rejected by the parties within five days.

Apparently for many years the arbitration process was viewed as only an early step in the negotiations. Pre-arbitral discussions were perfunctory and the arbitration decisions were often rejected. More recently the pre-arbitral discussions have been taken more seriously, and this has resulted in more agreements short of arbitration and a greater likelihood that the arbitration decision, if there is one, will be accepted.

2. *The Public Sector*

Advisory arbitration of grievances has frequently been used in the public sector as a compromise position between no arbitration and binding arbitration. The theory behind it is that an impartial ruling will convince the parties where the truth lies and thus facilitate a settlement. Some employees criticize advisory arbitration as inadequate because the employer retains the power to reject the decision. Some employers dislike it because it seems to be a foot in the door, a step toward binding arbitration. The former complaint seems unjustified, for most opinions are accepted in full and very few are completely rejected by the employer, either because the opinions are in fact convincing or because political pressures make rejection difficult. The latter fear, that advisory arbitration leads to binding arbitration, is more realistic, for many contracts do change in that direction. This does not necessarily prove that advisory arbitration is bad from an employer's point of view; to the contrary, it could simply indicate that the parties were satisfied enough to want to strengthen the procedure.

Fact-finding in public sector negotiation disputes grew out of the private sector experience with Railway Labor Act and Taft-Hartley Act fact-finding panels. Some 20 states now have fact-finding procedures in their public sector labor relations laws. These laws vary somewhat in detail, but they can be broken down into two categories, fact-finding without recommendations and fact-finding with recommendations.

Fact-finding without recommendations is premised on the notion that someone does not know the real facts of the situation and that proclamation of the truth by a respected neutral will somehow assist the parties in reaching a settlement. The notion is a dubious one, for several reasons. There is seldom just one set of "true" facts; usually there are many, and choosing among them requires a subjective decision. Moreover, the parties are almost certain to know the relevant facts before fact-finding, or at least the facts they are willing to admit are relevant. The public may not know those facts, but they may not learn them from fact-finding because many reports are given little publicity and many others are far too complicated to create a consensus strong enough to influence the parties. For these reasons, one scholar claims that fact-finding without recommendations "is about as useful as a martini without gin."

Fact-finding with recommendations looks much like ordinary arbitration, but there are two crucial differences: the recommendations are not based on a mutually-accepted document, and the recommendations can be rejected. Under this system the fact-finder is expected first to examine the factual data submitted by the parties, the bargaining history, and the relevant labor market, and then to formulate his recommendations with an eye toward persuasion, voluntary agreement, and acceptability. He is not expected to decide as a judge would, solely on the basis of the strength of the competing cases, and in this respect he has more flexibility than an arbitrator would. Strictly factual issues such as the wages paid to comparable employees in the area might be resolved as in binding arbitration, but policy questions like union security plans and automation proposals require more subtlety.

Where fact-finding has been in effect for some time the parties seem reasonably satisfied with it. One danger in the process is that unions might come to view the fact-finder's recommendations as a floor and then engage in further bargaining to raise that floor. This would in turn cause the parties to withhold their best offers in negotiations before fact-finding begins, and thus decrease the possibility of a voluntary settlement. To date this does not seem to have happened in many places.

D. INTEREST ARBITRATION

1. *In General*

Interest arbitration has much in common with two of the topics previously discussed, compulsory arbitration and fact-finding. All of these deal primarily with resolution of negotiation disputes, but interest arbitration is broader than either of the others because it is both voluntary and binding.

Although interest arbitration is today far less common than grievance arbitration, it was practiced long before grievance arbitration. Logically this had to be so because grievance arbitration presupposes a written agreement and a mature bargaining relationship, neither of which were common until relatively recent times. By contrast, what is now known as interest arbitration could be used even in the newest of relationships, particularly when the dispute is over a single issue such as wages. Thus arbitration was used to settle wage disputes in urban transit systems and coal mines as early as the turn of the century.

Interest arbitration became less popular as contracts became more complex, for parties were less confident that an outsider could decide difficult questions of policy and procedure than they were about a neutral's ability to choose between two wage scales. Interest arbitration was to some extent a victim of success of collective bargaining in another sense. As collective bargaining became familiar, parties to it were less likely to need a third party's advice.

It is ironic that after many years of neglect, interest arbitration is making something of a comeback in both the private and public sectors and among academic commentators as well.

2. The Private Sector

The Amalgamated Transit Union has used interest arbitration with great success for over seventy-five years. Early in their collective bargaining relationship the union and the transit companies recognized that the public suffered if they were unable to settle their disputes short of a work stoppage and chose interest arbitration as a way to avoid that problem. Today transit industry interest arbitration covers the full range of bargaining issues. The parties use a tripartite board which settles many issues voluntarily in executive session, almost as if it were an extension of negotiations rather than as an alternative to them. The transit industry has almost completely been taken over by local and state governments in the past two or three decades, but the arbitration system has remained intact, largely as a result of federal legislation conditioning federal aid on the preservation of transit employee collective bargaining rights. Critics of interest arbitration claim that it may become addictive and that parties may negotiate less seriously if arbitration is always available in lieu of a strike or lockout, but this has not happened in transit negotiations, most of which are settled far short of arbitration.

Large segments of the newspaper industry have used interest arbitration for many years. The first "International Arbitration Agreement" with the International Typographical Union was signed in 1901, and current contracts of the International Printing Pressmen with the American Newspaper Publishers Association also provide for interest arbitration. One unique aspect of the Pressmen's contract is that provision is made for appeal of local arbitration awards to yet another arbitration body, the International Arbitration Board, which is composed of three representatives each from labor and management and one neutral. There is some feeling on the part of management that the availability of appellate review destroys any hope of finality in the first arbitration award and thus causes unnecessary delay and expense, but this has not caused the parties to change their procedures.

By far the most significant recent advance in interest arbitration was the adoption of the Experimental Negotiating Agreement (ENA) by the United Steelworkers of America and the major steel producers in 1974. Unusual economic pressures forced the parties into this experiment.

Several times after World War II, negotiations between the union and the manufacturers on a new contract broke down and the resulting strike deprived many customer industries of the steel they needed. As a result, many customers built up large reserves of steel before the contract expiration date with the result that demand for steel was artificially inflated just before the expiration date and artificially deflated after a new contract was signed. This variation of demand prevented steady production at an optimum rate and cost the industry many millions of dollars. Other customers shifted purchases to foreign producers who could guarantee delivery, and many of those producers were able to demand (and get) long-term contracts that took a great deal of business away from American producers. Finally, there was a strong risk of government intervention in steel strikes, a prospect neither party welcomed.

Obviously both labor and management suffered from these problems, and in 1974 they decided to try a new approach. The ENA provided that if the parties were unable to resolve certain national issues in their next round of negotiations, they would turn them over to an arbitration panel for a final, binding determination. The panel was to consist of five members, one each from labor and management and three mutually selected neutrals, of whom two were required to be thoroughly familiar with steel production and its labor relations problems.

The ENA was warmly praised by outsiders but it was controversial within the union. Many union members viewed it, quite accurately, as a waiver of the employees' best weapon. Nevertheless, because the potential gains from the ENA were so large, because certain key items such as union security clauses were not subject to arbitration, and because locals of the Steelworkers remained free to strike on local issues, the leadership of the Steelworkers was able to overcome objections and renew the ENA in the 1977 contract. The ENA has not yet been used, and it remains to be seen whether it will be followed if negotiations do reach an impasse, and whether it would be renewed if it ever is used.

One unanswered question about private sector interest arbitration is whether agreements to arbitrate negotiation disputes are specifically enforceable. *Boys Markets* dealt only with grievance arbitration, and even that decision was limited by the holding in *Buffalo Forge* that an injunction would be appropriate only if the dispute is "over" an arbitrable issue. It might seem at first glance that a negotiation impasse constitutes such an arbitrable issue, but it should be remembered that *Boys Markets* was a narrow exception to the strong anti-injunction policies of the Norris-LaGuardia Act. A strong case can be made that

that exception is justified only by the preference for traditional grievance arbitration shown in later congressional enactments and ought not to be extended to include novelties like interest arbitration.

The Supreme Court has not yet addressed the issue, and the lower federal courts are sharply divided on this question. The earlier cases, like *Boston Printing Pressmen's Union v. Potter Press,* 141 F.Supp. 553 (D.Mass.1956), tended to hold that injunctions were not available. More recent cases, particularly those decided after *Boys Markets,* tend to hold the opposite. See, *e. g., Nashville Newspaper Printing Pressmen's Union, Local 50 v. Newspaper Printing Corp.,* 399 F.Supp. 593 (M.D. Tenn.1974), aff'd 518 F.2d 351 (6th Cir. 1975). The only case so far to address the question of the enforceability of the ENA did not provide a conclusive answer but did take an ominously narrow approach. The decision is unclear, but it seems to rest denial of an injunction on the facts that the instant dispute involved issues that were only arguably within the scope of the ENA and the agreement did not explicitly require arbitration of disputes over the coverage of the ENA itself. That being so, said the court, *Buffalo Forge* prohibits an injunction. *Coordinating Committee Steel Companies v. United Steelworkers of America,* 436 F. Supp. 208 (W.D.Pa.1977).

3. The Public Sector

Interest arbitration is a more recent phenomenon in the public sector, but it is already better established there than in the private sector. Much of what was said above in connection with compulsory arbitration in the public sector applies to interest arbitration. The reasons for and against interest arbitration are the same, as are the bases for state constitutional challenge (chiefly as an impermissible delegation of power) and the court responses thereto (varied, but generally allowing arbitration if decisional standards are expressed or implied).

A majority of the states using interest arbitration require exhaustion of mediation or fact-finding, or both, before arbitration is initiated to maximize the possibility of voluntary settlement. For the same reason, most states require the parties to bear at least part of the cost of arbitration but provide mediation assistance out of general state funds: the latter is thereby encouraged, and the former discouraged.

Beyond those generalities there is great flexibility among the various state laws, with wide differences in the administration of the statutes, processes for selecting the arbitrator or arbitrators (although most have settled on the tripartite board approach), the range of issues that may go to arbitration and the methods that may be used by the arbitrator.

Most state statutes specify some criteria to be used by interest arbitrators and a few have adopted the "final-offer" form (both of which are discussed below), but in other respects interest arbitration closely resembles grievance arbitration.

As one might expect, this variety of approaches has produced a wide range of results. One of the most notable results is that in Pennsylvania, where the statute makes arbitration easily available and does not require the exhaustion of intermediate bargaining steps, a greater percentage of negotiations proceeds to arbitration than in states where arbitration is less freely available.

4. *Criteria*

Perhaps the greatest difficulty in making interest arbitration work is selection of the appropriate criteria. In grievance arbitration there is, in rough terms, only a single criterion: what did the parties intend in their agreement, or if no intention is shown, what would they have intended had they thought about this question? In interest arbitration no single factor controls. In wage determinations, for example, comparability (wages paid to comparable employees elsewhere) will give some guidance, but so will ability of the employer to pay, recent changes in the cost of living, productivity changes, and many other things. Moreover, each of the relevant factors is complicated and subject to much debate. Is comparability of teachers' salaries to be determined by salaries in neighboring districts, by the county, state, or national averages, or by levels in certain districts that are themselves comparable? How are the employer's resources to be measured? What percentage of productivity savings should be devoted to wage increases and what percentage to tax decreases?

Notwithstanding these uncertainties, many contracts and statutes spell out criteria the arbitrator must apply. Some of these are very general, while others are quite specific. Typical of the latter is the Michigan statute covering police and firemen, which directs the arbitration panel to base its opinions on the following factors:

(a) The lawful authority of the employer.

(b) Stipulations of the parties.

(c) The interests and welfare of the public and the financial ability of the unit of government to meet those costs.

(d) Comparison of the wages, hours and conditions of employment of the employees involved in the arbitration proceeding with the wages, hours and conditions of employment of other employees performing similar services and with other employees generally:

(i) In public employment in comparable communities.

(ii) In private employment in comparable communities.

(e) The average consumer prices for goods and services, commonly known as the cost of living.

(f) The overall compensation presently received by the employees, including direct wage compensation, vacations, holidays and other excused time, insurance and pensions, medical and hospitalization benefits, the continuity and stability of employment, and all other benefits received.

(g) Changes in any of the foregoing circumstances during the pendency of the arbitration proceedings.

(h) Such other factors, not confined to the foregoing, which are normally or traditionally taken into consideration in the determination of wages, hours and conditions of employment through voluntary collective bargaining, mediation, fact-finding, arbitration or otherwise between the parties, in the public service or in private employment.

Each commentator has his own additions to or subtractions from that list, but one broad factor suggested by Professor Tim Bornstein should be kept in mind because it is operative whether stated or not. Arbitrators, says Bornstein, should and do give substantial weight to the wishes and aspirations of employees, the employer, and (in public sector cases) the community. Stated another way, the arbitration award should be **acceptable**—that is, not so far outside the range of the parties' reasonable expectations as to be foredoomed to rejection.

The most difficult problem is not in identifying the relevant criteria, but in ranking them, for inevitably they will be in conflict. An arbitrator may well be faced with a situation where comparability demands a substantial increase but the employer's ability to pay leaves little room for improvement. Related to this problem is the difficulty of weighing a mass of evidence that is contradictory or inconclusive. It is rare that the parties agree on "comparable wages" or on the magnitude of changes in the cost of living. It is far more common for them to have conflicting but equally well-documented positions, and it is the arbitrator's unenviable task to choose between them.

It should be clear from what has already been said that the interest arbitrator's role is not simply a judicial one. He must not simply try to determine what the parties "would have agreed on" had they bargained successfully, for their presence before him is conclusive evidence that they could not agree. Rather, his task is legislative in nature, to mandate a "fair" agreement based upon all of the relevant considerations.

5. *Final-Offer Arbitration*

How then does the arbitrator act legislatively and select a "fair" settlement? There is a natural tendency to regard the final positions of the parties as the parameters of a "fair" decision. As to wages, for example, the arbitrator could reasonably assume that the parties would be astounded if he set wages at a level below the employer's last offer or above the union's last offer. Moreover, there is a similar tendency to feel that the truth lies "somewhere in the middle," or to put it less kindly, there is a strong attraction to a "split-the-difference" approach.

Apart from the fact that the truth may not be midway between the parties' last positions, the "split-the-difference" mentality makes voluntary settlement less likely. If the arbitrator is likely to improve upon each party's last offer, the wise negotiator would not offer his "bottom line" figure to the other side because the arbitrator would then go beyond that figure. If he offers less than his limit, there is room for the arbitrator to move without going beyond what the party was willing to settle on. If both sides do this, they are less likely to enter into the range of agreement necessary for a voluntary settlement.

These fears may not be realistic, but they are real. In an attempt to avoid this problem a few states and municipalities have adopted a procedure termed final-offer arbitration. As the term im-

[*235*]

plies, this involves arbitration of negotiation disputes where the arbitrator chooses between the parties' final offers. (The "high-low" arbitration of baseball players' salaries discussed above is an example of final-offer arbitration.)

Final-offer arbitration proposals rest on the theory that each party to a negotiation will moderate and refine its positions to make its final offer as attractive as possible to the neutral. In the course of doing this, it is hoped, the parties will either find their final positions so close that a settlement will be reached before an arbitration award is rendered, or narrow the number and scope of the issues going to the arbitrator.

The theory is appealing but final offer arbitration does have some disadvantages. Arbitrators, as might be expected, are bothered by the lack of flexibility and the risk of being forced to choose between two unacceptable positions. More generally some commentators have pointed out that drafting a final offer requires a sophistication about arbitral standards many negotiators lack and that one or both parties may be forced for political reasons to include unfair or unjustified proposals (called "zingers") in their final offers with the attendant risk that these might be incorporated in the arbitrator's award.

There are several types of final offer systems. The two most notable are the Wisconsin system, which uses a single arbitrator who receives the final offers five days before the hearing and at its close must select one "package" or the other, and the Michigan system, which uses a tripartite panel which receives the final offers at any time up to the close of the hearing and selects between them on an issue-by-issue basis.

Early studies of these two models indicate that the Wisconsin system does a better job of bringing about settlements prior to arbitration and that the Michigan system tends to compel the arbitrator to engage in mediation during the hearing (resulting in a combination of mediation and arbitration, termed "med-arb"). Both systems work to the advantage of weak unions by reducing disparities between comparable communities. At least in Wisconsin neither management nor labor has benefitted disproportionately, for each has won about half of the arbitrations. Neither system has had the feared "narcotic effect" on the parties' collective bargaining efforts, for only a few negotiations result in arbitration.

APPENDIX 1

AMERICAN ARBITRATION ASSOCIATION FORMS

Form 1

AMERICAN ARBITRATION ASSOCIATION

VOLUNTARY LABOR ARBITRATION RULES

DEMAND FOR ARBITRATION

DATE:

TO: (Name) _____

(of party upon whom the Demand is made)

(Address) _____

(City and State) _____

The undersigned, a party to an arbitration agreement contained in a written contract, dated _____, providing for arbitration, hereby demands arbitration thereunder.

(attach arbitration clause or
quote hereunder)

NATURE OF DISPUTE:

REMEDY SOUGHT:

You are hereby notified that copies of our arbitration agreement and of this demand are being

[*238*]

filed with the American Arbitration Association
at its _____ Regional Office, with the request
that it commence the administration of the arbitration.

Signed _____

Title _____

Address _____

City and State _____

Telephone _____

To institute proceedings, please send three copies of this Demand with the administrative fee, as
provided in Section 43 of the Rules.

Form 2

AMERICAN ARBITRATION ASSOCIATION

SUBMISSION TO ARBITRATION

DATE:

The named Parties hereby submit the following dispute to arbitration under the VOLUNTARY LABOR ARBITRATION RULES of the American Arbitration Association:

We agree that we will abide by and perform any Award rendered hereunder and that a judgment may be entered upon the Award.

Employer _____

Signed by _____ Title _____

Address _____

Union _____ Local _____

Signed by _____ Title _____

Address _____

PLEASE FILE TWO COPIES

Form 3

AMERICAN ARBITRATION ASSOCIATION

Case Number: Date List Submitted:

LIST FOR SELECTION OF ARBITRATOR

After striking the
name of any
unacceptable
arbitrator, please
indicate your
order of prefer-
ence by number.
We will try to
appoint a mutually
acceptable arbitra-
tor who can hear
your case promptly.
Leave as many
names as possible.

_____

_____

_____

_____

_____

_____

_____

_____

_____

_____

_____

Party _____

By _____ Title _____

NOTE: Biographical information is attached. Unless your response is received by the Association by _____, all names submitted may be deemed acceptable. If a mutual selection cannot be made from this list, and if both parties do not request a further list, the Association may appoint an arbitrator.

The AAA's Award Bank includes published and unpublished awards of many of the arbitrators listed. Parties can write to the AAA's Publications Department for any arbitrator's recent awards. Copies will be provided at 30 cents per page.

Form 4

AMERICAN ARBITRATION ASSOCIATION

In the Matter of the
Arbitration between   Case Number:

Representatives:

NOTICE OF APPOINTMENT

TO:

YOU HAVE BEEN SELECTED as arbitrator in the above case. If you are able to accept this responsibility, please sign below and return.

The Code of Professional Responsibility for Arbitrators of Labor-Management Disputes requires certain disclosures so that the parties have complete confidence in the arbitrator's impartiality. Therefore, please disclose any current or past managerial, representational, or consultative relationship with the employer or labor organization involved in this proceeding, as well as any close personal relationship or other circumstances which might reasonably raise a question as to your impartiality. If you are serving concurrently as an advocate for or representative of parties in labor relations matters, or have done so in recent years, you should also disclose such

[243]

activities before accepting appointment. Disclosure must also be made of any pertinent pecuniary interest. If you are aware of any such relationship, please describe it on the back of this form. The AAA will call the facts to the attention of the parties.

ARBITRATOR'S OATH

STATE OF ⎱
COUNTY OF ⎰ SS.:

The undersigned, being duly sworn and being aware of the requirements for impartiality, hereby accepts this appointment and will faithfully and fairly hear and examine the matters in controversy between the above-named Parties, in accordance with the Arbitration Agreement that will be furnished by the Parties at the hearing, and will make a just Award according to the best of his or her understanding.

Signed _____

Arbitrator

Sworn to before me

this _____ day of _____ 19__.

NOTICE TO ARBITRATOR. Please execute and return one copy to this office.

Form 5

AMERICAN ARBITRATION ASSOCIATION

In the Matter of the Arbitration between

CASE NUMBER:

NOTICE OF HEARING

TO:

PLEASE TAKE NOTICE that a Hearing in the above-entitled Arbitration will be held at the Arbitration Tribunal of the American Arbitration Association,

At _____

Date _____

Hour _____

Before _____

_____

_____ Arbitrator(s)

Please attend promptly with your witnesses and be prepared to present your proofs.

DATED: _____

Tribunal Administrator

NOTICE: The Arbitrator(s) have arranged their schedule and reserved the above date to meet the convenience of the Parties. Therefore, every effort should be made to appear on the date scheduled. **In the event that unforeseen circumstances make it impossible to attend the hearing as scheduled, the Parties are to request a postponement no less than 48 hours before the time and date set for hearing. All requests for postponements must be communicated to the Tribunal Administrator (not the Arbitrator).** There should be no communication between Parties and the Arbitrator other than at oral hearings. Any party desiring to have a stenographic record of the testimony taken should make arrangements with the Tribunal Administrator in advance of the hearing.

cc: arbitrator(s)

Form 6

ARBITRATION TRIBUNALS OF THE AMERICAN ARBITRATION ASSOCIATION

In the Matter of the Arbitration between	Subpoena Duces Tecum (Documents)

THE PEOPLE OF THE STATE OF

To:

GREETING:

WE COMMAND YOU, that all business and excuses being laid aside, you and each of you appear and attend before

, Arbitrator(s) acting under the Arbitration Law of this State, at the American Arbitration Association, _____
(address)

on the _____ day of _____, 19__, at _____ o'clock to testify and give evidence in a certain Arbitration, then and there to be held between the above entitled parties, and that you bring with you and produce certain now in your custody.

Requested by: _____   Signed: _____

_____   Signed: _____

   Name of Attorney   Arbitrator(s)

_____

     Address

_____

    Telephone

Dated: _____

Form 7

AMERICAN ARBITRATION ASSOCIATION, ADMINISTRATOR

Voluntary Labor Arbitration Tribunal

In the Matter of the Arbitration between	**Stipulation**

IT IS HEREBY STIPULATED AND AGREED between the Parties to the above entitled Arbitration that

---

(Name of Party)

(Signed by)

(Title and Date)

(Name of Party)

(Signed by)

(Title and Date)

Case No. _____

Form 8

AMERICAN ARBITRATION ASSOCIATION

VOLUNTARY LABOR ARBITRATION TRIBUNAL

In the Matter of the Arbitration between

CASE NUMBER:

AWARD OF ARBITRATOR

THE UNDERSIGNED ARBITRATOR(S), having been designated in accordance with the arbitration agreement entered into by the above-named Parties, and dated _____ and having been duly sworn and having duly heard the proofs and allegations of the Parties, AWARDS as follows:

_____

Arbitrator's signature (dated)

STATE OF ⎫
          ⎬ ss.:
COUNTY OF ⎭

On this _____ day of _____, 19__, before me personally came and appeared _____ to me known and known to me to be the individual(s) described in and who executed the foregoing instrument and he acknowledged to me that he executed the same.

A.A.A. FORMS

Form 9

ARBITRATOR'S BILL

This bill is submitted on behalf of the Arbitrator

Make check payable and mail directly to Arbitrator

ARBITRATOR _____ Case No. _____

ADDRESS _____ No. of Grievances _____

_____

Appt. from List. ☐ Adm. ☐

UNION

EMPLOYER

To be filled out by the Arbitrator

ARBITRATOR'S COMPENSATION

Number of hearing days_____ @ $_____ $_____

Study and preparation days___ @ $_____ $_____

Other (specify) _____ @ $_____ $_____

FEE TOTAL $_____

ARBITRATOR'S EXPENSES

Transportation $_____

Hotel $_____

Meals $_____

Other (specify) $_____ $_____

TOTAL $_____

Payable by Employer $_____

Payable by Union $_____

Arbitrator's S.S. No. _____

Date _____ Signature _____

AAA Signature _____

DO NOT PAY UNLESS AAA SIGNATURE IS AFFIXED

APPENDIX 2

AAA VOLUNTARY LABOR ARBITRATION RULES

1. **Agreement of Parties**—The parties shall be deemed to have made these Rules a part of their arbitration agreement whenever, in a collective bargaining agreement or submission, they have provided for arbitration by the American Arbitration Association (hereinafter AAA) or under its Rules. These Rules shall apply in the form obtaining at the time the arbitration is initiated.

2. **Name of Tribunal**—Any Tribunal constituted by the parties under these Rules shall be called the Voluntary Labor Arbitration Tribunal.

3. **Administrator**—When parties agree to arbitrate under these Rules and an arbitration is instituted thereunder, they thereby authorize the AAA to administer the arbitration. The authority and obligations of the Administrator are as provided in the agreement of the parties and in these Rules.

4. **Delegation of Duties**—The duties of the AAA may be carried out through such representatives or committees as the AAA may direct.

5. **National Panel of Labor Arbitrators**—The AAA shall establish and maintain a National

Panel of Labor Arbitrators and shall appoint arbitrators therefrom, as hereinafter provided.

6. **Office of Tribunal**—The general office of the Labor Arbitration Tribunal is the headquarters of the AAA, which may, however, assign the administration of an arbitration to any of its Regional Offices.

7. **Initiation Under an Arbitration Clause in a Collective Bargaining Agreement**—Arbitration under an arbitration clause in a collective bargaining agreement under these Rules may be initiated by either party in the following manner:

(a) By giving written notice to the other party of intention to arbitrate (Demand), which notice shall contain a statement setting forth the nature of the dispute and the remedy sought, and

(b) By filing at any Regional Office of the AAA three copies of said notice, together with a copy of the collective bargaining agreement, or such parts thereof as relate to the dispute, including the arbitration provisions. After the Arbitrator is appointed, no new or different claim may be submitted to him except with the consent of the Arbitrator and all other parties.

8. **Answer**—The party upon whom the Demand for Arbitration is made may file an answering

statement with the AAA within seven days after notice from the AAA, in which event he shall simultaneously send a copy of his answer to the other party. If no answer is filed within the stated time, it will be assumed that the claim is denied. Failure to file an answer shall not operate to delay the arbitration.

9. **Initiation Under a Submission**—Parties to any collective bargaining agreement may initiate an arbitration under these Rules by filing at any Regional Office of the AAA two copies of a written agreement to arbitrate under these Rules (Submission), signed by the parties and setting forth the nature of the dispute and the remedy sought.

10. **Fixing of Locale**—The parties may mutually agree upon the locale where the arbitration is to be held. If the locale is not designated in the collective bargaining agreement or Submission, and if there is a dispute as to the appropriate locale, the AAA shall have the power to determine the locale and its decision shall be binding.

11. **Qualifications of Arbitrator**—No person shall serve as a neutral Arbitrator in any arbitration in which he has any financial or personal interest in the result of the arbitration, unless the parties, in writing, waive such disqualification.

12. **Appointment from Panel**—If the parties have not appointed an Arbitrator and have not provid-

ed any other method of appointment, the Arbitrator shall be appointed in the following manner: Immediately after the filing of the Demand or Submission, the AAA shall submit simultaneously to each party an identical list of names of persons chosen from the Labor Panel. Each party shall have seven days from the mailing date in which to cross off any names to which he objects, number the remaining names indicating the order of his preference, and return the list to the AAA. If a party does not return the list within the time specified, all persons named therein shall be deemed acceptable. From among the persons who have been approved on both lists, and in accordance with the designated order of mutual preference, the AAA shall invite the acceptance of an Arbitrator to serve. If the parties fail to agree upon any of the persons named or if those named decline or are unable to act, or if for any other reason the appointment cannot be made from the submitted lists, the Administrator shall have the power to make the appointment from other members of the Panel without the submission of any additional lists.

13. **Direct Appointment by Parties**—If the agreement of the parties names an Arbitrator or specifies a method of appointing an Arbitrator, that designation or method shall be followed. The notice of appointment, with the name and address

of such Arbitrator, shall be filed with the AAA by the appointing party.

If the agreement specifies a period of time within which an Arbitrator shall be appointed, and any party fails to make such appointment within that period, the AAA may make the appointment.

If no period of time is specified in the agreement, the AAA shall notify the parties to make the appointment and if within seven days thereafter such Arbitrator has not been so appointed, the AAA shall make the appointment.

14. **Appointment of Neutral Arbitrator by Party-Appointed Arbitrators**—If the parties have appointed their Arbitrators, or if either or both of them have been appointed as provided in Section 13, and have authorized such Arbitrators to appoint a neutral Arbitrator within a specified time and no appointment is made within such time or any agreed extension thereof, the AAA may appoint a neutral Arbitrator, who shall act as Chairman.

If no period of time is specified for appointment of the neutral Arbitrator and the parties do not make the appointment within seven days from the date of the appointment of the last party-appointed Arbitrator, the AAA shall appoint such neutral Arbitrator, who shall act as Chairman.

If the parties have agreed that the Arbitrators shall appoint the neutral Arbitrator from the Panel, the AAA shall furnish to the party-appointed Arbitrators, in the manner prescribed in Section 12, a list selected from the Panel, and the appointment of the neutral Arbitrator shall be made as prescribed in such Section.

15. **Number of Arbitrators**—If the arbitration agreement does not specify the number of Arbitrators, the dispute shall be heard and determined by one Arbitrator, unless the parties otherwise agree.

16. **Notice to Arbitrator of His Appointment**— Notice of the appointment of the neutral Arbitrator shall be mailed to the Arbitrator by the AAA and the signed acceptance of the Arbitrator shall be filed with the AAA prior to the opening of the first hearing.

17. **Disclosure by Arbitrator of Disqualification** —Prior to accepting his appointment, the prospective neutral Arbitrator shall disclose any circumstances likely to create a presumption of bias or which he believes might disqualify him as an impartial Arbitrator. Upon receipt of such information, the AAA shall immediately disclose it to the parties. If either party declines to waive the presumptive disqualification, the vacancy thus created shall be filled in accordance with the applicable provisions of these Rules.

18. **Vacancies**—If any Arbitrator should resign, die, withdraw, refuse or be unable or disqualified to perform the duties of his office, the AAA shall, on proof satisfactory to it, declare the office vacant. Vacancies shall be filled in the same manner as that governing the making of the original appointment, and the matter shall be reheard by the new Arbitrator.

19. **Time and Place of Hearing**—The Arbitrator shall fix the time and place for each hearing. At least five days prior thereto the AAA shall mail notice of the time and place of hearing to each party, unless the parties otherwise agree.

20. **Representation by Counsel**—Any party may be represented at the hearing by counsel or by other authorized representative.

21. **Stenographic Record**—Any party may request a stenographic record by making arrangements for same through the AAA. If such transcript is agreed by the parties to be, or in appropriate cases determined by the Arbitrator to be the official record of the proceeding, it must be made available to the Arbitrator, and to the other party for inspection, at a time and place determined by the Arbitrator. The total cost of such a record shall be shared equally by those parties that order copies.

22. **Attendance at Hearings**—Persons having a direct interest in the arbitration are entitled to

attend hearings. The Arbitrator shall have the power to require the retirement of any witness or witnesses during the testimony of other witnesses. It shall be discretionary with the Arbitrator to determine the propriety of the attendance of any other persons.

23. **Adjournments**—The Arbitrator for good cause shown may adjourn the hearing upon the request of a party or upon his own initiative, and shall adjourn when all the parties agree thereto.

24. **Oaths**—Before proceeding with the first hearing, each Arbitrator may take an Oath of Office, and if required by law, shall do so. The Arbitrator may, in his discretion, require witnesses to testify under oath administered by any duly qualified person, and if required by law or requested by either party, shall do so.

25. **Majority Decision**—Whenever there is more than one Arbitrator, all decisions of the Arbitrators shall be by majority vote. The award shall also be made by majority vote unless the concurrence of all is expressly required.

26. **Order of Proceedings**—A hearing shall be opened by the filing of the Oath of the Arbitrator, where required, and by the recording of the place, time and date of hearing, the presence of the Arbitrator and parties, and counsel if any, and the receipt by the Arbitrator of the Demand and answer, if any, or the Submission.

[*259*]

Exhibits, when offered by either party, may be received in evidence by the Arbitrator. The names and addresses of all witnesses and exhibits in order received shall be made a part of the record.

The Arbitrator may, in his discretion, vary the normal procedure under which the initiating party first presents his claim, but in any case shall afford full and equal opportunity to all parties for presentation of relevant proofs.

27. **Arbitration in the Absence of a Party**—Unless the law provides to the contrary, the arbitration may proceed in the absence of any party, who, after due notice, fails to be present or fails to obtain an adjournment. An award shall not be made solely on the default of a party. The Arbitrator shall require the other party to submit such evidence as he may require for the making of an award.

28. **Evidence**—The parties may offer such evidence as they desire and shall produce such additional evidence as the Arbitrator may deem necessary to an understanding and determination of the dispute. When the Arbitrator is authorized by law to subpoena witnesses and documents, he may do so upon his own initiative or upon the request of any party. The Arbitrator shall be the judge of the relevancy and materiality of the evidence offered and conformity to legal rules of evidence shall not be necessary. All evidence

shall be taken in the presence of all of the Arbitrators and all of the parties except where any of the parties is absent in default or has waived his right to be present.

29. **Evidence by Affidavit and Filing of Documents**—The Arbitrator may receive and consider the evidence of witnesses by affidavit, but shall give it only such weight as he deems proper after consideration of any objections made to its admission.

All documents not filed with the Arbitrator at the hearing but which are arranged at the hearing or subsequently by agreement of the parties to be submitted, shall be filed with the AAA for transmission to the Arbitrator. All parties shall be afforded opportunity to examine such documents.

30. **Inspection**—Whenever the Arbitrator deems it necessary, he may make an inspection in connection with the subject matter of the dispute after written notice to the parties who may, if they so desire, be present at such inspection.

31. **Closing of Hearings**—The Arbitrator shall inquire of all parties whether they have any further proofs to offer or witnesses to be heard. Upon receiving negative replies, the Arbitrator shall declare the hearings closed and a minute thereof shall be recorded. If briefs or other documents are to be filed, the hearings shall be declared closed as of the final date set by the Arbi-

trator for filing with the AAA. The time limit within which the Arbitrator is required to make his award shall commence to run, in the absence of other agreement by the parties, upon the closing of the hearings.

32. **Reopening of Hearings**—The hearings may be reopened by the Arbitrator on his own motion, or on the motion of either party, for good cause shown, at any time before the award is made, but if the reopening of the hearing would prevent the making of the award within the specific time agreed upon by the parties in the contract out of which the controversy has arisen, the matter may not be reopened, unless both parties agree upon the extension of such time limit. When no specific date is fixed in the contract, the Arbitrator may reopen the hearings, and the Arbitrator shall have 30 days from the closing of the reopened hearings within which to make an award.

33. **Waiver of Rules**—Any party who proceeds with the arbitration after knowledge that any provision or requirement of these Rules has not been complied with and who fails to state his objection thereto in writing, shall be deemed to have waived his right to object.

34. **Waiver of Oral Hearings**—The parties may provide, by written agreement, for the waiver of oral hearings. If the parties are unable to agree

as to the procedure, the AAA shall specify a fair and equitable procedure.

35. **Extensions of Time**—The parties may modify any period of time by mutual agreement. The AAA for good cause may extend any period of time established by these Rules, except the time for making the award. The AAA shall notify the parties of any such extension of time and its reason therefor.

36. **Serving of Notices**—Each party to a Submission or other agreement which provides for arbitration under these Rules shall be deemed to have consented and shall consent that any papers, notices or process necessary or proper for the initiation or continuation of an arbitration under these Rules and for any court action in connection therewith or the entry of judgment on an award made thereunder, may be served upon such party (a) by mail addressed to such party or his attorney at his last known address, or (b) personal service, within or without the state wherein the arbitration is to be held.

37. **Time of Award**—The award shall be rendered promptly by the Arbitrator and, unless otherwise agreed by the parties, or specified by the law, not later than 30 days from the date of closing the hearings, or if oral hearings have been waived, then from the date of transmitting the final statements and proofs to the Arbitrator.

38. **Form of Award**—The award shall be in writing and shall be signed either by the neutral Arbitrator or by a concurring majority if there be more than one Arbitrator. The parties shall advise the AAA whenever they do not require the Arbitrator to accompany the award with an opinion.

39. **Award Upon Settlement**—If the parties settle their dispute during the course of the arbitration, the Arbitrator, upon their request, may set forth the terms of the agreed settlement in an award.

40. **Delivery of Award to Parties**—Parties shall accept as legal delivery of the award the placing of the award or a true copy thereof in the mail by the AAA, addressed to such party at his last known address or to his attorney, or personal service of the award, or the filing of the award in any manner which may be prescribed by law.

41. **Release of Documents for Judicial Proceedings**—The AAA shall, upon the written request of a party, furnish to such party at his expense certified facsimiles of any papers in the AAA's possession that may be required in judicial proceedings relating to the arbitration.

42. **Judicial Proceedings**—The AAA is not a necessary party in judicial proceedings relating to the arbitration.

43. **Administrative Fee**—As a nonprofit organization, the AAA shall prescribe an administrative fee schedule to compensate it for the cost of providing administrative services. The schedule in effect at the time of filing shall be applicable.

44. **Expenses**—The expense of witnesses for either side shall be paid by the party producing such witnesses.

Expenses of the arbitration, other than the cost of the stenographic record, including required traveling and other expenses of the Arbitrator and of AAA representatives, and the expenses of any witnesses or the cost of any proofs produced at the direct request of the Arbitrator, shall be borne equally by the parties unless they agree otherwise, or unless the Arbitrator in his award assesses such expenses or any part thereof against any specified party or parties.

45. **Communication with Arbitrator**—There shall be no communication between the parties and a neutral Arbitrator other than at oral hearings. Any other oral or written communications from the parties to the Arbitrator shall be directed to the AAA for transmittal to the Arbitrator.

46. **Interpretation and Application of Rules**—The Arbitrator shall interpret and apply these Rules insofar as they relate to his powers and duties. When there is more than one Arbitrator

and a difference arises among them concerning the meaning or application of any such Rules, it shall be decided by majority vote. If that is unobtainable, either Arbitrator or party may refer the question to the AAA for final decision. All other Rules shall be interpreted and applied by the AAA.

APPENDIX 3

AMERICAN ARBITRATION ASSOCIATION EXPEDITED LABOR ARBITRATION RULES

1. **Agreement of Parties**—These Rules shall apply whenever the parties have agreed to arbitrate under them, in the form obtaining at the time the arbitration is initiated.

2. **Appointment of Neutral Arbitrator**—The AAA shall appoint a single neutral Arbitrator from its Panel of Labor Arbitrators, who shall hear and determine the case promptly.

3. **Initiation of Expedited Arbitration Proceeding**—Cases may be initiated by joint submission in writing, or in accordance with a collective bargaining agreement.

4. **Qualifications of Neutral Arbitrator**—No person shall serve as a neutral Arbitrator in any arbitration in which that person has any financial or personal interest in the result of the arbitration. Prior to accepting an appointment, the prospective Arbitrator shall disclose any circumstances likely to prevent a prompt hearing or to create a presumption of bias. Upon receipt of such information, the AAA shall immediately replace that Arbitrator or communicate the information to the parties.

5. **Vacancy**—The AAA is authorized to substitute another Arbitrator if a vacancy occurs or if an appointed Arbitrator is unable to serve promptly.

6. **Time and Place of Hearing**—The AAA shall fix a mutually convenient time and place of the hearing, notice of which must be given at least 24 hours in advance. Such notice may be given orally.

7. **Representation by Counsel**—Any party may be represented at the hearing by counsel or other representative.

8. **Attendance at Hearings**—Persons having a direct interest in the arbitration are entitled to attend hearings. The Arbitrator may require the retirement of any witness during the testimony of other witnesses. The Arbitrator shall determine whether any other person may attend the hearing.

9. **Adjournments**—Hearings shall be adjourned by the Arbitrator only for good cause, and an appropriate fee will be charged by the AAA against the party causing the adjournment.

10. **Oaths**—Before proceeding with the first hearing, the Arbitrator shall take an oath of office. The Arbitrator may require witnesses to testify under oath.

11. **No Stenographic Record**—There shall be no stenographic record of the proceedings.

12. **Proceedings**—The hearing shall be conducted by the Arbitrator in whatever manner will most expeditiously permit full presentation of the evidence and the arguments of the parties. The Arbitrator shall make an appropriate minute of the proceedings. Normally, the hearing shall be completed within one day. In unusual circumstances and for good cause shown, the Arbitrator may schedule an additional hearing, within five days.

13. **Arbitration in the Absence of a Party**—The arbitration may proceed in the absence of any party who, after due notice, fails to be present. An award shall not be made solely on the default of a party. The Arbitrator shall require the attending party to submit supporting evidence.

14. **Evidence**—The Arbitrator shall be the sole judge of the relevancy and materiality of the evidence offered.

15. **Evidence by Affidavit and Filing of Documents**—The Arbitrator may receive and consider evidence in the form of an affidavit, but shall give appropriate weight to any objections made. All documents to be considered by the Arbitrator shall be filed at the hearing. There shall be no post hearing briefs.

16. **Close of Hearings**—The Arbitrator shall ask whether parties have any further proofs to offer or witnesses to be heard. Upon receiving negative replies, the Arbitrator shall declare and note the hearing closed.

17. **Waiver of Rules**—Any party who proceeds with the arbitration after knowledge that any provision or requirement of these Rules has not been complied with and who fails to state his objections thereto in writing shall be deemed to have waived his right to object.

18. **Serving of Notices**—Any papers or process necessary or proper for the initiation or continuation of an arbitration under these Rules and for any court action in connection therewith or for the entry of judgment on an Award made thereunder, may be served upon such party (a) by mail addressed to such party or its attorney at its last known address, or (b) by personal service, or (c) as otherwise provided in these Rules.

19. **Time of Award**—The award shall be rendered promptly by the Arbitrator and, unless otherwise agreed by the parties, not later than five business days from the date of the closing of the hearing.

20. **Form of Award**—The Award shall be in writing and shall be signed by the Arbitrator. If the Arbitrator determines that an opinion is necessary, it shall be in summary form.

21. **Delivery of Award to Parties**—Parties shall accept as legal delivery of the award the placing of the award or a true copy thereof in the mail by the AAA, addressed to such party at its last known address or to its attorney, or personal service of the award, or the filing of the award in any manner which may be prescribed by law.

22. **Expenses**—The expenses of witnesses for either side shall be paid by the party producing such witnesses.

23. **Interpretation and Application of Rules**—The Arbitrator shall interpret and apply these Rules insofar as they relate to his powers and duties. All other Rules shall be interpreted and applied by the AAA, as Administrator.

APPENDIX 4

FEDERAL MEDIATION AND CON-
CILIATION SERVICE
(29 CFR Part 1404)

ARBITRATION SERVICES

SUBPART A: ARBITRATION POLICY; AD-
MINISTRATION OF ROSTER

1404.1 Scope and Authority

This chapter is issued by the Federal Mediation and Conciliation Service (FMCS) under Title II of the Labor Management Relations Act of 1947 (Public Law 80–101) as amended in 1959 (Public Law 86–257) and 1974 (Public Law 93–360). The chapter applies to all arbitrators listed on the FMCS Roster of Arbitrators, to all applicants for listing on the Roster, and to all persons or parties seeking to obtain from FMCS either names or panels of names of arbitrators listed on the Roster in connection with disputes which are to be submitted to arbitration or fact-finding.

1404.2 Policy

The labor policy of the United States is designed to promote the settlement of issues between employers and represented employees through the processes of collective bargaining and voluntary arbitration. This policy encourages the use of voluntary arbitration to resolve disputes over the interpretation or application of collective bargaining agreements. Voluntary arbitration and fact-finding in disputes and disagreements over establishment or modification of contract terms are important features of constructive labor-management relations, as alternatives to economic strife in the settlement of labor disputes.

1404.3 Administrative Responsibilities

(a) *Director*. The Director of FMCS has ultimate responsibility for all aspects of FMCS arbitration activities and is the final agency authority on all questions concerning the Roster or FMCS arbitration procedures.

(b) *Office of Arbitration Services*. The Office of Arbitration Services (OAS) maintains a Roster of Arbitrators (the "Roster"); administers Subpart C of these Regulations (Procedures for Arbitration Services); assists, promotes, and cooperates in the establishment of programs for training and developing new arbitrators; collects information and statistics concerning the arbitration function, and performs other tasks in connection with the function that may be assigned by the Director.

(c) *Arbitrator Review Board*. The Arbitrator Review Board (the "Board") shall consist of a presiding officer and such members and alternate members as the Director may appoint, and who shall serve at the Director's pleasure and may be removed at any time. The Board shall be composed entirely of full-time officers or employees of the Federal Government. The Board shall establish its own procedures for carrying out its duties.

(1) *Duties of the Board.* The Board shall:

(i) Review the qualifications of all applicants for listing on the Roster, interpreting and applying the criteria set forth in subsection 1404.5 of this part;

(ii) Review the status of all persons whose continued eligibility for listing on the Roster has been questioned under subsection 1404.5 of this part;

(iii) Make recommendations to the Director regarding acceptance or rejection of applicants for listing on the Roster, or regarding withdrawal of listing on the Roster for any of the reasons set forth herein.

SUBPART B: ROSTER OF ARBITRATORS; ADMISSION AND RETENTION

1404.4 Roster and Status of Members

(a) *The Roster.* The FMCS shall maintain a Roster of labor arbitrators consisting of persons who meet the criteria for listing contained in subsection 1404.5 of this part and whose names have not been removed from the Roster in accordance with subsection 1404.5(d).

(b) *Adherence to Standards and Requirements*. Persons listed on the Roster shall comply with the FMCS rules and regulations pertaining to arbitration and with such guidelines and procedures as may be issued by OAS pursuant to Subpart C hereof. Arbitrators are also expected to conform to the ethical standards and procedures set forth in the Code of Professional Responsibility for Arbitrators of Labor Management Disputes, as approved by the Joint Steering Committee of the National Academy of Arbitrators.

(c) *Status of Arbitrators*. Persons who are listed on the Roster and are selected or appointed to hear arbitration matters or to serve as factfinders do not become employees of the Federal Government by virtue of their selection or appointment. Following selection or appointment, the arbitrator's relationship is solely with the parties to the dispute, except that arbitrators are subject to certain reporting requirements and to standards of conduct as set forth in this Part.

(d) *Role of FMCS*. FMCS has no power to:

(1) Compel parties to arbitrate or agree to arbitration;

(2) Enforce an agreement to arbitrate;

(3) Compel parties to agree to a particular arbitrator;

(4) Influence, alter or set aside decisions of arbitrators listed on the Roster;

(5) Compel, deny or modify payment of compensation to an arbitrator.

(e) *Nominations and Panels.* On request of the parties to an agreement to arbitrate or engage in fact-finding, or where arbitration or fact-finding may be provided for by statute, OAS will provide names or panels of names without charge. Procedures for obtaining these services are contained in Subpart C. Neither the submission of a nomination or panel nor the appointment of an arbitrator constitutes a determination by FMCS that an agreement to arbitrate or enter fact-finding proceedings exists; nor does such action constitute a ruling that the matter in controversy is arbitrable under any agreement.

(f) *Rights of Persons Listed on the Roster.* No person shall have any right to be listed or to remain listed on the Roster. FMCS retains the authority and responsibility to assure that the needs of the parties using its facilities are served. To accomplish this purpose it may establish procedures for the preparation of panels or the appointment of arbitrators or fact finders which include consideration of such factors as background and experience, availability, acceptability, geographical location and the expressed preferences of the parties.

1404.5 Listing on the Roster; Criteria for Listing and Retention

Persons seeking to be listed on the Roster must complete and submit an application form which may be obtained from the Office of Arbitration Services. Upon receipt of an executed form, OAS will review the application, assure that it is complete, make such inquiries as are necessary, and submit the application to the Arbitrator Review Board. The Board will review the completed applications under the criteria set forth in subsections (a), (b) and (c) of this Section, and will forward to the Director its recommendation on each applicant. The Director makes all final decisions as to whether an applicant may be listed. Each applicant shall be notified in writing of the Director's decision and the reasons therefore.

(a) *General Criteria.* Applicants for the Roster will be listed on the Roster upon a determination that they:

(1) Are experienced, competent and acceptable in decision-making roles in the resolution of labor relations disputes; or

(2) Have extensive experience in relevant positions in collective bargaining; and

(3) Are capable of conducting an orderly hearing, can analyze testimony and exhibits and can prepare clear and concise findings and awards within reasonable time limits.

[277]

(b) *Proof of Qualification.* The qualifications listed in (a) above are preferably demonstrated by the submission of actual arbitration awards prepared by the applicant while serving as an impartial arbitrator chosen by the parties to disputes. Equivalent experience acquired in training internship or other development programs, or experience such as that acquired as a hearing officer or judge in labor relations controversies may also be considered by the Board.

(c) *Advocacy.*

(1) *Definition.* An advocate is a person who represents employers, labor organizations, or individuals as an employee, attorney or consultant, in matters of labor relations, including but not limited to the subjects of union representation and recognition matters, collective bargaining, arbitration, unfair labor practices, equal employment opportunity and other areas generally recognized as constituting labor relations. The definition includes representatives of employers or employees in individual cases or controversies involving workmen's compensation, occupational health or safety, minimum wage or other labor standards matters. The definition of advocate also includes a person who is directly associated with an advocate in a business or professional relationship as, for example, partners or employees of a law firm.

(2) Eligibility. Except in the case of persons listed on the Roster before November 17, 1976, no person who is an advocate, as defined above, may be listed. No person who was listed on the Roster at any time who was not an advocate when listed or who did not divulge advocacy at the time of listing may continue to be listed after becoming an advocate or after the fact of advocacy is revealed.

(d) *Duration of Listing, Retention.* Initial listing may be for a period not to exceed three years, and may be renewed thereafter for periods not to exceed two years, provided upon review that the listing is not canceled by the Director as set forth below. Notice of cancellation may be given to the member whenever the member:

(1) No longer meets the criteria for admission;

(2) Has been repeatedly and flagrantly delinquent in submitting awards;

(3) Has refused to make reasonable and periodic reports to FMCS, as required in Subpart C, concerning activities pertaining to arbitration;

(4) Has been the subject of complaints by parties who use FMCS facilities and the Director, after appropriate inquiry, concludes

that just cause for cancellation has been shown.

(5) Is determined by the Director to be unacceptable to the parties who use FMCS arbitration facilities; the Director may base a determination of unacceptability on FMCS records showing the number of times the arbitrator's name has been proposed to the parties and the number of times it has been selected.

No listing may be cancelled without at least sixty days notice of the reasons for the proposed removal, unless the Director determines that the FMCS or the parties will be harmed by continued listing. In such cases an arbitrator's listing may be suspended without notice or delay pending final determination in accordance with these procedures. The member shall in either case have an opportunity to submit a written response showing why the listing should not be cancelled. The Director may, at his discretion, appoint a hearing officer to conduct an inquiry into the facts of any proposed cancellation and to make recommendations to the Director.

1404.6 Freedom of Choice

Nothing contained herein should be construed to limit the rights of parties who use FMCS arbitration facilities jointly to select any arbitrator or arbitration procedure acceptable to them.

SUBPART C: PROCEDURES FOR ARBITRATION SERVICES

1404.10 Procedures for Requesting Arbitration Panels

The Office of Arbitration Services has been delegated the responsibility for administering all requests for arbitration services under these regulations.

(a) The Service will refer a panel of arbitrators to the parties upon request. The Service prefers to act upon a joint request which should be addressed to the Federal Mediation and Conciliation Service, Washington, D. C. 20427, Attention: Office of Arbitration Services. In the event that the request is made by only one party, the Service will submit a panel; however, any submission of a panel should not be construed as anything more than compliance with a request and does not necessarily reflect the contractual requirements of the parties.

(b) The parties are urged to use the Request for Arbitration Panel form (R–43) which has been prepared by the Service and is available in quantity at all FMCS regional offices and field stations or upon request to the Office of Arbitration Services, 2100 K Street, Washington, D. C. 20427. The form R–43 is reproduced herein for purposes of identification.

(c) A brief statement of the issues in dispute should accompany the request to enable the Service to submit the names of arbitrators qualified for the issues involved. The request should also include a current copy of the arbitration section of the collective bargaining agreement or stipulation to arbitrate.

(d) If form R–43 is not utilized, the parties may request a panel by letter which must include the names, addresses, and phone numbers of the parties, the location of the contemplated hearing, the issue in dispute, the number of names desired on the panel, the industry involved and any special qualifications of the panel or special requirement desired.

1404.11   Arbitrability

Where either party claims that a dispute is not subject to arbitration, the Service will not decide the merit of such claim.

1404.12   Nominations of Arbitrators

(a) When the parties have been unable to agree on an arbitrator, the Service will submit to the parties on request the names of seven arbitrators unless the applicable collective bargaining agreement provides for a different number, or unless the parties themselves request a different number. Together with the submission of a panel of arbitrators, the Service will furnish a biographical sketch for each member of the panel. This sketch states the background, qualifications, experience, and per diem fee established by the arbitrator. It states the existence, if any, of other fees such as cancellation, postponement, rescheduling, or administrative fees.

(b) When a panel is submitted, an FMCS control case number is assigned. All future communication between the parties and the Service should refer to the case number.

(c) The Service considers many factors when selecting names for inclusion on a panel, but the agreed-upon wishes of the parties are paramount. Special qualifications of arbitrators experienced in certain issues or industries, or possessing certain backgrounds, may be identified for purposes of submitting panels to accommodate the parties. The Service may also consider such things as general acceptability, geographical location, general experience, availability, size of fee, and the need to expose new arbitrators to the selection process in preparing panels. The Service has no obligation to put an individual on any given panel, or on a minimum number of panels in any fixed period, such as a month or a year.

(1) If at any time both parties request for valid reason, that a name or names be omitted from a panel, such name or names will be omitted, unless they are excessive in number.

(2) If at any time both parties request that a name or names be included on a panel, such name or names will be included.

(3) If only one party requests that a name or names be omitted from a panel, or that specific individuals be added to the panel, such request shall not be honored.

(4) If the issue described in the request appears to require special technical experience or qualifications, arbitrators who possess such qualifications will, where possible, be included on the panel submitted to the parties.

(5) In almost all cases, an arbitrator is chosen from one panel. However, if either party requests another panel, the Service shall comply with the request providing that an additional panel is permissible under the terms of the agreement or the other party so agrees. Requests for more than two panels must be accompanied by a statement of explanation and will be considered on a case-by-case basis.

1404.13 Selection and Appointment of Arbitrators

(a) The parties should notify the OAS of their selection of an arbitrator. The arbitrator, upon notification by the parties, shall notify the OAS of his selection and willingness to serve. Upon notification of the parties' selection of an arbitrator, the Service will make a formal appointment of the arbitrator.

(b) Where the contract is silent on the manner of selecting arbitrators, the parties may wish to consider one of the following methods for selection of an arbitrator from a panel:

(1) Each party alternately strikes a name from the submitted panel until one remains.

(2) Each party advises the Service of its order of preference by numbering each name on the panel and submitting the numbered list in writing to OAS. The name on the panel that has the lowest accumulated numerical number will be appointed.

(3) Informal agreement of the parties by whatever method they choose.

(c) The Service will, on joint or unilateral request of the parties, submit a panel or, when the applicable collective bargaining agreement authorizes, will make a direct appointment of an arbitrator. Submission of a panel or name signifies nothing more than compliance with a request and in no way constitutes a determination by the Service that the parties are obligated to arbitrate the dispute in question. Resolution of disputes as to the propriety of such a submission or appointment rests solely with the parties.

(d) The arbitrator, upon notification of appointment, is required to communicate with the parties immediately to arrange for preliminary matters, such as date and place of hearing.

1404.14 Conduct of Hearings

All proceedings conducted by the arbitrator shall be in conformity with the contractual obligations of the parties. The arbitrator is also expected to conduct all proceedings in conformity with Section 1404.4(b). The conduct of the arbitration proceeding is under the arbitrator's jurisdiction and control and the arbitrator's decision is to be based upon the evidence and testimony presented at the hearing or otherwise incorporated in the record of the proceeding. The arbitrator may, unless prohibited by law, proceed in the absence of any party who, after due notice, fails to be present or to obtain a postponement. An award rendered in an *ex parte* proceeding of this nature must be based upon evidence presented to the arbitrator.

1404.15 Decision and Award

(a) Arbitrators are encouraged to render awards not later than 60 days from the date of the closing of the record as determined by the arbitrator, unless otherwise agreed upon by the parties or specified by law. A failure to render timely awards reflects upon the performance of an arbitrator and may lead to his removal from the FMCS Roster.

(b) The parties should inform the OAS whenever a decision is unduly delayed. The arbitrator shall notify the OAS if and when the arbitrator (1) cannot schedule, hear and determine issues promptly, or (2) learns a dispute has been settled by the parties prior to the decision.

(c) After an award has been submitted to the parties the arbitrator is required to file a copy with the OAS. The arbitrator is further required to submit a Fee and Award Statement, form R–19, showing a breakdown of the fee and expense charges so that the Service may be in a position to review conformance with stated charges under 1404.12(a). Filing both award and report within 15 days after rendering an award is required of all arbitrators. The reports are not used for the purpose of compelling payment of fees.

(d) While the Service encourages the publication of arbitration awards, it is the policy of the Service not to release arbitration decisions for publication without the consent of both parties. Furthermore, the Service expects the arbitrators it has nominated or appointed not to give publicity to awards they issue if objected to by one of the parties.

1404.16   Fees and Charges of Arbitrators

(a) No administrative or filing fee is charged by the Service. The current policy of the Service permits each of its nominees or appointees to charge a per diem fee and other predetermined fees for services, the amount of which has been certified in advance to the Service. Each arbitrator's maximum per diem fee and the existence of other predetermined fees, if any, are set forth on a biographical sketch which is sent to the parties when panels are submitted and are the controlling fees. The arbitrator shall not change any fee or add charges without giving at least 30 days advance notice to the Service.

(b) In cases involving unusual amounts of time and expenses relative to pre-hearing and post-hearing administration of a particular case, an administrative charge may be made by the arbitrator.

(c) All charges other than those specified by 1404.16(a) shall be divulged to and agreement obtained by the arbitrator with the parties immediately after appointment.

(d) The Service requests that it be notified of any arbitrator's deviation from the policies expressed herein. However, the Service will not attempt to resolve any fee dispute.

1404.17 Reports and Biographical Sketches

(a) Arbitrators listed on the Roster shall execute and return all documents, forms and reports required by the Service. They shall also keep the Service informed of changes of address, telephone number, availability, and of any business or other connection or relationship which involves labor-management relations, or which creates or gives the appearance of advocacy as defined in Section 1404.4(c)(1).

(b) The Service may require each arbitrator listed on the Roster to prepare at the time of initial listing, and to revise, biographical information in accordance with a format to be provided by the Service at the time of initial listing or biennial review. Arbitrators may also request revision of biographical information at other times to reflect changes in fees, the existence of additional charges, address, experience and background, or other relevant data. The Service reserves the right to decide and approve the format and content of biographical sketches.

CODE OF PROFESSIONAL RESPONSI-BILITY FOR ARBITRATORS OF LA-BOR–MANAGEMENT DISPUTES OF THE NATIONAL ACADEMY OF AR-BITRATORS, THE AMERICAN AR-BITRATION ASSOCIATION, AND THE FEDERAL MEDIATION AND CONCILIATION SERVICE

FOREWORD

This "Code of Professional Responsibility for Arbitrators of Labor-Management Disputes" supersedes the "Code of Ethics and Procedural Standards for Labor-Management Arbitration," approved in 1951 by a Committe of the American Arbitration Association, by the National Academy of Arbitrators, and by representatives of the Federal Mediation and Conciliation Service.

Revision of the 1951 Code was initiated officially by the same three groups in October, 1972. The Joint Steering Committee named below was designated to draft a proposal.

Reasons for Code revision should be noted briefly. Ethical considerations and procedural standards are sufficiently intertwined to warrant combining the subject matter of Part I and II of the 1951 Code under the caption of "Professional Responsibility." It has seemed advisable to eliminate admonitions to the parties (Part III of the 1951 Code) except as they appear incidentally in connection with matters primarily involving responsibilities of arbitrators. Substantial growth of third party participation in dispute resolution in the public sector requires consideration. It appears that arbitration of new contract terms may become more significant. Finally, during the interval of more than two decades, new problems have emerged as private sector grievance arbitration has matured and has become more diversified.

JOINT STEERING COMMITTEE

Chairman
William E. Simkin

Representing American Arbitration Association
Frederick H. Bullen
Donald B. Straus

Representing Federal Mediation and Conciliation Service
Lawrence B. Babcock, Jr.
L. Lawrence Schultz

Representing National Academy of Arbitrators
Sylvester Garrett
Ralph T. Seward   *November 30, 1974*

TABLE OF CONTENTS

6. POST HEARING CONDUCT
    A. Post Hearing Briefs and Submissions
    B. Disclosure of Terms of Award
    C. Awards and Opinions
    D. Clarification or Interpretation of Awards
    E. Enforcement of Award

PREAMBLE

Background

Voluntary arbitration rests upon the mutual desire of management and labor in each collective bargaining relationship to develop procedures for dispute settlement which meet their own particular needs and obligations. No two voluntary systems, therefore, are likely to be identical in practice. Words used to describe arbitrators (Arbitrator, Umpire, Impartial Chairman, Chairman of Arbitration Board, etc.) may suggest typical approaches but actual differences within any general type of arrangement may be as great as distinctions often made among the several types.

Some arbitration and related procedures, however, are not the product of voluntary agreement. These procedures, primarily but not exclusively applicable in the public sector, sometimes utilize other third party titles (Fact Finder, Impasse Panel, Board of Inquiry, etc.). These procedures range all the way from arbitration prescribed by statute to arrangements substantially indistinguishable from voluntary procedures.

The standards of professional responsibility set forth in this Code are designed to guide the impartial third party serving in these diverse labor-management relationships.

Scope of Code

This Code is a privately developed set of standards of professional behavior. It applies to voluntary arbitration of labor-management grievance disputes and of disputes concerning new or revised contract terms. Both "ad hoc" and "permanent" varieties of voluntary arbitration, private and public sector, are included. To the extent relevant in any specific case, it also applies to advisory arbitration, impasse resolution panels, arbitration prescribed by statutes, fact-finding, and other special procedures.

The word "arbitrator," as used hereinafter in the Code, is intended to apply to any impartial person, irrespective of specific title, who serves in a labor-management dispute procedure in which there is conferred authority to decide issues or to make formal recommendations.

The Code is not designed to apply to mediation or conciliation, as distinguished from arbitration, nor to other procedures in which the third party is not authorized in advance to make decisions or recommendations. It does not apply to partisan representatives on tripartite boards. It does not apply to commercial arbitration or to other uses of arbitration outside the labor-management dispute area.

Format of Code

Bold Face type, sometimes including explanatory material, is used to set forth general principles. *Italics* are used for amplification of general principles. Ordinary type is used primarily for illustrative or explanatory comment.

Application of Code

Faithful adherence by an arbitrator to this Code is basic to professional responsibility.

The National Academy of Arbitrators will expect its members to be governed in their professional conduct by this Code and stands ready, through its Committee on Ethics and Grievances, to advise its members as to the Code's interpretation. The American Arbitration Association and the Federal Mediation and Conciliation Service will apply the Code to the arbitrators on their rosters in cases handled under their respective appointment or referral procedures. Other arbitrators and administrative agencies may, of course, voluntarily adopt the Code and be governed by it.

In interpreting the Code and applying it to charges of professional misconduct, under existing or revised procedures of the National Academy of Arbitrators and of the administrative agencies, it should be recognized that while some of its standards express ethical principles basic to the arbitration profession, others rest less on ethics than on considerations of good practice. Experience has shown the difficulty of drawing rigid lines of distinction between ethics and good practice and this Code does not attempt to do so. Rather, it leaves the gravity of alleged misconduct and the extent to which ethical standards have been violated to be assessed in the light of the facts and circumstances of each particular case.

1

ARBITRATOR'S QUALIFICATIONS AND RESPONSIBILITIES TO THE PROFESSION

A.   GENERAL QUALIFICATIONS

1.   Essential personal qualifications of an arbitrator include honesty, integrity, impartiality and general competence in labor relations matters.

An arbitrator must demonstrate ability to exercise these personal qualities faithfully and with good judgment, both in procedural matters and in substantive decisions.

a.   Selection by mutual agreement of the parties or direct designation by an administrative agency are the effective methods of appraisal of this combination of an individual's potential and performance, rather than

[*296*]

the fact of placement on a roster of an administrative agency or membership in a professional association of arbitrators.

2. An arbitrator must be as ready to rule for one party as for the other on each issue, either in a single case or in a group of cases. Compromise by an arbitrator for the sake of attempting to achieve personal acceptability is unprofessional.

B. QUALIFICATIONS FOR SPECIAL CASES

1. An arbitrator must decline appointment, withdraw, or request technical assistance when he or she decides that a case is beyond his or her competence.

a. An arbitrator may be qualified generally but not for specialized assignments. Some types of incentive, work standard, job evaluation, welfare program, pension, or insurance cases may require specialized knowledge, experience or competence. Arbitration of contract terms also may require distinctive background and experience.

b. Effective appraisal by an administrative agency or by an arbitrator of the need for special qualifications requires that both parties make known the special nature of the case prior to appointment of the arbitrator.

C. Responsibilities to the Profession

1. An arbitrator must uphold the dignity and integrity of the office and endeavor to provide effective service to the parties.

a. To this end, an arbitrator should keep current with principles, practices and developments that are relevant to his or her own field of arbitration practice.

2. An experienced arbitrator should cooperate in the training of new arbitrators.

3. An arbitrator must not advertise or solicit arbitration assignments.

a. It is a matter of personal preference whether an arbitrator includes "Labor Arbitrator" or similar notation on letterheads, cards, or announcements. *It is inappropriate, however, to include memberships or offices held in professional societies or listings on rosters of administrative agencies.*

b. *Information provided for published biographical sketches, as well as that supplied to administrative agencies, must be accurate.* Such information may include membership in professional organizations (including reference to significant offices held), and listings on rosters of administrative agencies.

2
RESPONSIBILITIES TO THE PARTIES

A. RECOGNITION OF DIVERSITY IN ARBITRATION ARRANGEMENTS

1. An arbitrator should conscientiously endeavor to understand and observe, to the extent consistent with professional responsibility, the significant principles governing each arbitration system in which he or she serves.

> a. Recognition of special features of a particular arbitration arrangement can be essential with respect to procedural matters and may influence other aspects of the arbitration process.

2. Such understanding does not relieve an arbitrator from a corollary responsibility to seek to discern and refuse to lend approval or consent to any collusive attempt by the parties to use arbitration for an improper purpose.

B. REQUIRED DISCLOSURES

1. Before accepting an appointment, an arbitrator must disclose directly or through the administrative agency involved, any current or past managerial, representational, or consultative relationship with any company or union involved in a proceeding in which he or she is being considered

for appointment or has been tentatively designated to serve. Disclosure must also be made of any pertinent pecuniary interest.

> a. The duty to disclose includes membership on a Board of Directors, full-time or part-time service as a representative or advocate, consultation work for a fee, current stock or bond ownership (other than mutual fund shares or appropriate trust arrangements) or any other pertinent form of managerial, financial or immediate family interest in the company or union involved.

2. When an arbitrator is serving concurrently as an advocate for or representative of other companies or unions in labor relations matters, or has done so in recent years, he or she must disclose such activities before accepting appointment as an arbitrator.

An arbitrator must disclose such activities to an administrative agency if he or she is on that agency's active roster or seeks placement on a roster. Such disclosure then satisfies this requirement for cases handled under that agency's referral.

> a. It is not necessary to disclose names of clients or other specific details. It is necessary to indicate the general nature of the labor relations advocacy or representa-

tional work involved, whether for companies or unions or both, and a reasonable approximation of the extent of such activity.

b. *An arbitrator on an administrative agency's roster has a continuing obligation to notify the agency of any significant changes pertinent to this requirement.*

c. When an administrative agency is not involved, an arbitrator must make such disclosure directly unless he or she is certain that both parties to the case are fully aware of such activities.

3. An arbitrator must not permit personal relationships to affect decision-making.

Prior to acceptance of an appointment, an arbitrator must disclose to the parties or to the administrative agency involved any close personal relationship or other circumstance, in addition to those specifically mentioned earlier in this section, which might reasonably raise a question as to the arbitrator's impartiality.

a. Arbitrators establish personal relationships with many company and union representatives, with fellow arbitrators, and with fellow members of various professional associations. There should be no attempt to be secretive about such friendships or acquaintances but disclosure is not necessary unless some feature of a particular relationship might reasonably appear to impair impartiality.

4. If the circumstances requiring disclosure are not known to the arbitrator prior to acceptance of appointment, disclosure must be made when such circumstances become known to the arbitrator.

5. The burden of disclosure rests on the arbitrator. After appropriate disclosure, the arbitrator may serve if both parties so desire. If the arbitrator believes or perceives that there is a clear conflict of interest, he or she should withdraw, irrespective of the expressed desires of the parties.

C. Privacy of Arbitration

1. All significant aspects of an arbitration proceeding must be treated by the arbitrator as confidential unless this requirement is waived by both parties or disclosure is required or permitted by law.

a. Attendance at hearings by persons not representing the parties or invited by either or both of them should be permitted only when the parties agree or when an applicable law requires or permits. Occasionally, special circumstances may require that an arbitrator rule on such matters as attendance and degree of participation of counsel selected by a grievant.

b. *Discussion of a case at any time by an arbitrator with persons not involved directly should be limited to situations where advance approval or consent of both parties is obtained or where the identity of the parties and details of the case are sufficiently obscured to eliminate any realistic probability of identification.*

A commonly recognized exception is discussion of a problem in a case with a fellow arbitrator. *Any such discussion does not relieve the arbitrator who is acting in the case from sole responsibility for the decision and the discussion must be considered as confidential.*

Discussion of aspects of a case in a classroom without prior specific approval of the parties is not a violation provided the arbitrator is satisfied that there is no breach of essential confidentiality.

c. *It is a violation of professional responsibility for an arbitrator to make public an award without the consent of the parties.*

An arbitrator may request but not press the parties for consent to publish an opinion. Such a request should normally not be made until after the award has been issued to the parties.

d. It is not improper for an arbitrator to donate arbitration files to a library of a college, university or similar institution without prior consent of all the parties involved. When the circumstances permit, there should be deleted from such donations any cases concerning which one or both of the parties have expressed a desire for privacy. As an additional safeguard, an arbitrator may also decide to withhold recent cases or indicate to the donee a time interval before such cases can be made generally available.

e. *Applicable laws, regulations, or practices of the parties may permit or even require exceptions to the above noted principles of privacy.*

D. PERSONAL RELATIONSHIPS WITH THE PARTIES

1. An arbitrator must make every reasonable effort to conform to arrangements required by an administrative agency or mutually desired by the parties regarding communications and personal relationships with the parties.

a. *Only an "arm's-length" relationship may be acceptable to the parties in some arbitration arrangements or may be required by the rules of an administrative agency. The arbitrator should then have no contact of consequence with representatives of either party while handling a case without the other party's presence or consent.*

b. In other situations, both parties may want communications and personal relationships to be less formal. It is then appropriate for the arbitrator to respond accordingly.

E.   JURISDICTION

1.   **An arbitrator must observe faithfully both the limitations and inclusions of the jurisdiction conferred by an agreement or other submission under which he or she serves.**

2.   **A direct settlement by the parties of some or all issues in a case, at any stage of the proceedings, must be accepted by the arbitrator as relieving him or her of further jurisdiction over such issues.**

F.   MEDIATION BY AN ARBITRATOR

1.   **When the parties wish at the outset to give an arbitrator authority both to mediate and to decide or submit recommendations regarding residual issues, if any, they should so advise the arbitrator prior to appointment.   If the appointment is accepted, the arbitrator must perform a mediation role consistent with the circumstances of the case.**

a. Direct appointments, also, may require a dual role as mediator and arbitrator of residual issues. This is most likely to occur in some public sector cases.

2. When a request to mediate is first made after appointment, the arbitrator may either accept or decline a mediation role.

a. *Once arbitration has been invoked, either party normally has a right to insist that the process be continued to decision.*

b. *If one party request that the arbitrator mediate and the other party objects, the arbitrator should decline the request.*

c. *An arbitrator is not precluded from making a suggestion that he or she mediate. To avoid the possibility of improper pressure, the arbitrator should not so suggest unless it can be discerned that both parties are likely to be receptive. In any event, the arbitrator's suggestion should not be pursued unless both parties readily agree.*

G. RELIANCE BY AN ARBITRATOR ON OTHER ARBITRATION AWARDS OR ON INDEPENDENT RESEARCH

1. An arbitrator must assume full personal responsibility for the decision in each case decided.

a. *The extent, if any, to which an arbitrator properly may rely on precedent, on guidance of other awards, or on independent research is dependent primarily on the policies of the parties on these matters, as expressed in the contract, or other agreement, or at the hearing.*

b.   When the mutual desires of the parties are not known or when the parties express differing opinions or policies, the arbitrator may exercise discretion as to these matters, consistent with acceptance of full personal responsibility for the award.

H.   Use of Assistants

1.   An arbitrator must not delegate any decision-making function to another person without consent of the parties.

a.   *Without prior consent of the parties, an arbitrator may use the services of an assistant for research, clerical duties, or preliminary drafting under the direction of the arbitrator, which does not involve the delegation of any decision-making function.*

b.   *If an arbitrator is unable, because of time limitations or other reasons, to handle all decision-making aspects of a case, it is not a violation of professional responsibility to suggest to the parties an allocation of responsibility between the arbitrator and an assistant or associate.   The arbitrator must not exert pressure on the parties to accept such a suggestion.*

I. Consent Awards

1. Prior to issuance of an award, the parties may jointly request the arbitrator to include in the award certain agreements between them, concerning some or all of the issues. If the arbitrator believes that a suggested award is proper, fair, sound, and lawful, it is consistent with professional responsibility to adopt it.

a. Before complying with such a request, an arbitrator must be certain that he or she understands the suggested settlement adequately in order to be able to appraise its terms. If it appears that pertinent facts or circumstances may not have been disclosed, the arbitrator should take the initiative to assure that all significant aspects of the case are fully understood. To this end, the arbitrator may request additional specific information and may question witnesses at a hearing.

J. Avoidance of Delay

1. It is a basic professional responsibility of an arbitrator to plan his or her work schedule so that present and future commitments will be fulfilled in a timely manner.

a. *When planning is upset for reasons beyond the control of the arbitrator, he or she, nevertheless, should exert every reasonable effort to fulfill all commitments. If this is not possible, prompt notice at the arbitrator's initiative should be given to all parties affected. Such notices should include reasonably accurate estimates of any additional time required. To the extent possible, priority should be given to cases in process so that other parties may make alternative arbitration arrangements.*

2. **An arbitrator must cooperate with the parties and with any administrative agency involved in avoiding delays.**

a. *An arbitrator on the active roster of an administrative agency must take the initiative in advising the agency of any scheduling difficulties that he or she can foresee.*

b. *Requests for services, whether received directly or through an administrative agency, should be declined if the arbitrator is unable to schedule a hearing as soon as the parties wish. If the parties, nevertheless, jointly desire to obtain the services of the arbitrator and the arbitrator agrees, arrangements should be made by agreement that the arbitrator confidently expects to fulfill.*

c. *An arbitrator may properly seek to persuade the parties to alter or eliminate arbitration procedures or tactics that cause unnecessary delay.*

3. **Once the case record has been closed, an arbitrator must adhere to the time limits for an award, as stipulated in the labor agreement or as provided by regulation of an administrative agency or as otherwise agreed.**

a. *If an appropriate award cannot be rendered within the required time, it is incumbent on the arbitrator to seek an extension of time from the parties.*

b. *If the parties have agreed upon abnormally short time limits for an award after a case is closed, the arbitrator should be so advised by the parties or by the administrative agency involved, prior to acceptance of appointment.*

K. Fees and Expenses

1. **An arbitrator occupies a position of trust in respect to the parties and the administrative agencies. In charging for services and expenses, the arbitrator must be governed by the same high standards of honor and integrity that apply to all other phases of his or her work.**

An arbitrator must endeavor to keep total charges for services and expenses reasonable and

consistent with the nature of the case or cases decided.

Prior to appointment, the parties should be aware of or be able readily to determine all significant aspects of an arbitrator's bases for charges for fees and expenses.

a. *Services Not Primarily Chargeable on a Per Diem Basis*

By agreement with the parties, the financial aspects of many "permanent" arbitration assignments, of some interest disputes, and of some "ad hoc" grievance assignments do not include a per diem fee for services as a primary part of the total understanding. *In such situations, the arbitrator must adhere faithfully to all agreed-upon arrangements governing fees and expenses.*

b. *Per Diem Basis for Charges for Services*

(1) *When an arbitrator's charges for services are determined primarily by a stipulated per diem fee, the arbitrator should establish in advance his or her bases for application of such per diem fee and for determination of reimbursable expenses.*

Practices established by an arbitrator should include the basis for charges, if any, for:

(a) hearing time, including the application of the stipulated basic per diem hearing fee to hearing days of varying lengths;

(b) study time;

(c) necessary travel time when not included in charges for hearing time;

(d) postponement or cancellation of hearings by the parties and the circumstances in which such charges will normally be assessed or waived;

(e) office overhead expenses (secretarial, telephone, postage, etc.);

(f) the work of paid assistants or associates.

(2) *Each arbitrator should be guided by the following general principles:*

(a) *Per diem charges for a hearing should not be in excess of actual time spent or allocated for the hearing.*

(b) *Per diem charges for study time should not be in excess of actual time spent.*

(c) *Any fixed ratio of study days to hearing days, not agreed to specifically by the parties, is inconsistent with the per diem method of charges for services.*

(d) Charges for expenses must not be in excess of actual expenses normally reimbursable and incurred in connection with the case or cases involved.

(e) When time or expense are involved for two or more sets of parties on the same day or trip, such time or expense charges should be appropriately prorated.

(f) An arbitrator may stipulate in advance a minimum charge for a hearing without violation of (a) or (e) above.

(3) An arbitrator on the active roster of an administrative agency must file with the agency his or her individual bases for determination of fees and expenses if the agency so requires. Thereafter, it is the responsibility of each such arbitrator to advise the agency promptly of any change in any basis for charges.

Such filing may be in the form of answers to a questionnaire devised by an agency or by any other method adopted by or approved by an agency.

Having supplied an administrative agency with the information noted above, an arbitrator's professional responsibility of disclosure under this Code with respect to fees and expenses has been satisfied for cases referred by that agency.

(4) *If an administrative agency promulgates specific standards with respect to any of these matters which are in addition to or more restrictive than an individual arbitrator's standards, an arbitrator on its active roster must observe the agency standards for cases handled under the auspices of that agency, or decline to serve.*

(5) *When an arbitrator is contacted directly by the parties for a case or cases, the arbitrator has a professional responsibility to respond to questions by submitting his or her bases for charges for fees and expenses.*

(6) *When it is known to the arbitrator that one or both of the parties cannot afford normal charges, it is consistent with professional responsibility to charge lesser amounts to both parties or to one of the parties if the other party is made aware of the difference and agrees.*

(7) *If an arbitrator concludes that the total of charges derived from his or her*

normal basis of calculation is not compatible with the case decided, it is consistent with professional responsibility to charge lesser amounts to both parties.

2. An arbitrator must maintain adequate records to support charges for services and expenses and must make an accounting to the parties or to an involved administrative agency on request.

3
RESPONSIBILITIES TO ADMINISTRATIVE AGENCIES

A. GENERAL RESPONSIBILITIES

1. An arbitrator must be candid, accurate, and fully responsive to an administrative agency concerning his or her qualifications, availability, and all other pertinent matters.

2. An arbitrator must observe policies and rules of an administrative agency in cases referred by that agency.

3. An arbitrator must not seek to influence an administrative agency by any improper means, including gifts or other inducements to agency personnel.

a. It is not improper for a person seeking placement on a roster to request references from individuals having knowledge of the applicant's experience and qualifications.

b. Arbitrators should recognize that the primary responsibility of an administrative agency is to serve the parties.

4
PREHEARING CONDUCT

1. All prehearing matters must be handled in a manner that fosters complete impartiality by the arbitrator.

a. The primary purpose of prehearing discussions involving the arbitrator is to obtain agreement on procedural matters so that the hearing can proceed without unnecessary obstacles. If differences of opinion should arise during such discussions and, particularly, if such differences appear to impinge on substantive matters, the circumstances will suggest whether the matter can be resolved informally or may require a prehearing conference or, more rarely, a formal preliminary hearing. When an administrative agency handles some or all aspects of the arrangements prior to a hearing, the arbitrator will become involved only if differences of some substance arise.

b. *Copies of any prehearing correspondence between the arbitrator and either party must be made available to both parties.*

5
HEARING CONDUCT

A.   GENERAL PRINCIPLES

1.   An arbitrator must provide a fair and adequate hearing which assures that both parties have sufficient opportunity to present their respective evidence and argument.

    a.   *Within the limits of this responsibility, an arbitrator should conform to the various types of hearing procedures desired by the parties.*

    b.   An arbitrator may: encourage stipulations of fact; restate the substance of issues or arguments to promote or verify understanding; question the parties' representatives or witnesses, when necessary or advisable, to obtain additional pertinent information; and request that the parties submit additional evidence, either at the hearing or by subsequent filing.

    c.   *An arbitrator should not intrude into a party's presentation so as to prevent that party from putting forward its case fairly and adequately.*

B. Transcripts or Recordings

1. Mutual agreement of the parties as to use or non-use of a transcript must be respected by the arbitrator.

a. *A transcript is the official record of a hearing only when both parties agree to a transcript or an applicable law or regulation so provides.*

b. An arbitrator may seek to persuade the parties to avoid use of a transcript, or to use a transcript if the nature of the case appears to require one. *However, if an arbitrator intends to make his or her appointment to a case contingent on mutual agreement to a transcript, that requirement must be made known to both parties prior to appointment.*

c. If the parties do not agree to a transcript, an arbitrator may permit one party to take a transcript at its own cost. The arbitrator may also make appropriate arrangements under which the other party may have access to a copy, if a copy is provided to the arbitrator.

d. Without prior approval, an arbitrator may seek to use his or her own tape recorder to supplement note taking. The arbitrator should not insist on such a tape recording if either or both parties object.

C. Ex Parte Hearings

1. **In determining whether to conduct an ex parte hearing, an arbitrator must consider relevant legal, contractual, and other pertinent circumstances.**

2. **An arbitrator must be certain, before proceeding ex parte, that the party refusing or failing to attend the hearing has been given adequate notice of the time, place, and purposes of the hearing.**

D. Plant Visits

1. **An arbitrator should comply with a request of any party that he or she visit a work area pertinent to the dispute prior to, during, or after a hearing. An arbitrator may also initiate such a request.**

> a. *Procedures for such visits should be agreed to by the parties in consultation with the arbitrator.*

E. Bench Decisions or Expedited Awards

1. **When an arbitrator understands, prior to acceptance of appointment, that a bench decision is expected at the conclusion of the hearing, the arbitrator must comply with the understanding unless both parties agree otherwise.**

a. *If notice of the parties' desire for a bench decision is not given prior to the arbitrator's acceptance of the case, issuance of such a bench decision is discretionary.*

b. *When only one party makes the request and the other objects, the arbitrator should not render a bench decision except under most unusual circumstances.*

2. **When an arbitrator understands, prior to acceptance of appointment, that a concise written award is expected within a stated time period after the hearing, the arbitrator must comply with the understanding unless both parties agree otherwise.**

6
POST HEARING CONDUCT

A. POST HEARING BRIEFS AND SUBMISSIONS

1. **An arbitrator must comply with mutual agreements in respect to the filing or nonfiling of post hearing briefs or submissions.**

a. An arbitrator, in his or her discretion, may either suggest the filing of post hearing briefs or other submissions or suggest that none be filed.

b. When the parties disagree as to the need for briefs, an arbitrator may permit filing but may determine a reasonable time limitation.

2. An arbitrator must not consider a post hearing brief or submission that has not been provided to the other party.

B. DISCLOSURE OF TERMS OF AWARD

1. An arbitrator must not disclose a prospective award to either party prior to its simultaneous issuance to both parties or explore possible alternative awards unilaterally with one party, unless both parties so agree.

  a. Partisan members of tripartite boards may know prospective terms of an award in advance of its issuance. Similar situations may exist in other less formal arrangements mutually agreed to by the parties. In any such situation, the arbitrator should determine and observe the mutually desired degree of confidentiality.

C. AWARDS AND OPINIONS

1. The award should be definite, certain, and as concise as possible.

  a. When an opinion is required, factors to be considered by an arbitrator include: desirability of brevity, consistent with the nature of the case and any expressed desires of the parties; need to use a style and form that is understandable to responsible representatives of the parties, to the grievant and supervisors, and to others in the collective bargaining relationship; necessity of meeting the significant issues; forthrightness to an extent not harmful to the relationship of the parties; and avoidance of gratuitous advice or discourse not essential to disposition of the issues.

D.   Clarification or Interpretation
of Awards

1.   No clarification or interpretation of an award is permissible without the consent of both parties.

2.   Under agreements which permit or require clarification or interpretation of an award, an arbitrator must afford both parties an opportunity to be heard.

E.   Enforcement of Award

1.   The arbitrator's responsibility does not extend to the enforcement of an award.

2.   In view of the professional and confidential nature of the arbitration relationship, an arbitrator should not voluntarily participate in legal enforcement proceedings.

APPENDIX 6

THE UNITED STATES ARBITRATION ACT
(9 U.S.C.A. § 1–14)

CHAPTER 1.—GENERAL PROVISIONS

§ 1. "Maritime Transactions" and "Commerce" Defined; Exceptions to Operation of Title

"Maritime transactions," as herein defined, means charter parties, bills of lading of water carriers, agreements relating to wharfage, supplies furnished vessels or repairs of vessels, collisions, or any other matters in foreign commerce which, if the subject of controversy, would be embraced within admiralty jurisdiction; "commerce," as herein defined, means commerce among the several States or with foreign nations, or in any Territory of the United States or in the District of Columbia, or between any such Territory and another, or between any such Territory and any State or foreign nation, or between the District of Columbia and any State or Territory or foreign nation, but nothing herein contained shall apply to contracts of employment of seamen, railroad employees, or any other class of workers engaged in foreign or interstate commerce.

§ 2. Validity, Irrevocability, and Enforcement of Agreements to Arbitrate

A written provision in any maritime transaction or a contract evidencing a transaction involving commerce to settle by arbitration a controversy thereafter arising out of such contract or transaction, or the refusal to perform the whole or any part thereof, or an agreement in writing to submit to arbitration an existing controversy arising out of such a contract, transaction, or refusal, shall be valid, irrevocable, and enforceable, save upon such grounds as exist at law or in equity for the revocation of any contract.

§ 3. Stay of Proceedings Where Issue Therein Referable to Arbitration

If any suit or proceeding be brought in any of the courts of the United States upon any issue referable to arbitration under an agreement in writing for such arbitration, the court in which such suit is pending, upon being satisfied that the issue involved in such suit or proceeding is referable to arbitration under such an agreement, shall on application of one of the parties stay the trial of the action until such arbitration has been had in accordance with the terms of the agreement, providing the applicant for the stay is not in default in proceeding with such arbitration.

§ 4. Failure to Arbitrate Under Agreement; Petition to United States Court Having Jurisdiction for Order to Compel Arbitration; Notice and Service Thereof; Hearing and Determination

A party aggrieved by the alleged failure, neglect, or refusal of another to arbitrate under a written agreement for arbitration may petition any United States district court which, save for such agreement, would have jurisdiction under Title 28, in a civil action or in admiralty of the subject matter of a suit arising out of the controversy between the parties, for an order directing that such arbitration proceed in the manner provided for in such agreement. Five days' notice in writing of such application shall be served upon the party in default. Service thereof shall be made in the manner provided by the Federal Rules of Civil Procedure. The court shall hear the parties, and upon being satisfied that the making of the agreement for arbitration or the failure to comply therewith is not in issue, the court shall make an order directing the parties to proceed to arbitration in accordance with the terms of the agreement. The hearing and proceedings, under such agreement, shall be within the district in which the petition for an order directing such arbitration is filed. If the making of the arbitration agreement or the failure, neglect, or refusal to perform the same be in issue, the court shall proceed summarily to the trial thereof. If no jury trial be demanded by the party alleged to be in default, or if the matter in dispute is within admiralty jurisdiction, the court shall hear and determine such issue. Where such an issue is raised, the party alleged to be in default may, except in cases of admiralty, on or before the return day of the notice of application, demand a jury trial of such issue, and upon such demand the court shall make an order referring the issue or issues to a jury in the manner provided by the Federal Rules of Civil Procedure, or may specially call a jury for that purpose. If the jury find that no agreement in writing for arbitration was made or that there is no default in proceeding thereunder, the proceeding shall be dismissed. If the jury find that an agreement for arbitration was made in writing and that there is a default in proceeding thereunder, the court shall make an order summarily directing the parties to proceed with the arbitration in accordance with the terms thereof.

§ 5. **Appointment of Arbitrators or Umpire**

If in the agreement provision be made for a method of naming or appointing an arbitrator or arbitrators or an umpire, such method shall be followed; but if no method be provided therein, or if a method be provided and any party thereto shall fail to avail himself of such method, or if for any other reason there shall be a lapse in the naming of an arbitrator or arbitrators or umpire, or in filling a vacancy, then upon the application of either party to the controversy the court shall designate and appoint an arbitrator or arbitrators or umpire, as the case may require, who shall act under the said agreement with the same force and effect as if he or they had been specifically named therein; and unless otherwise provided in the agreement the arbitration shall be by a single arbitrator.

§ 6. **Application Heard as Motion**

Any application to the court hereunder shall be made and heard in the manner provided by law for the making and hearing of motions, except as otherwise herein expressly provided.

§ 7. **Witnesses Before Arbitrators; Fees; Compelling Attendance**

The arbitrators selected either as prescribed in this title or otherwise, or a majority of them, may summon in writing any person to attend before them or any of them as a witness and in a proper case to bring with him or them any book, record, document, or paper which may be deemed material as evidence in the case. The fees for such attendance shall be the same as the fees of witnesses before masters of the United States courts. Said summons shall issue in the name of the arbitrator or arbitrators, or a majority of them, and shall be signed by the arbitrators, or a majority of them, and shall be directed to the said person and shall be served in the same manner as subpoenas to appear and testify before the court; if any person or persons so summoned to testify shall refuse or neglect to obey said summons, upon petition the United States court in and for the district in which such arbitrators, or a majority of them, are sitting may compel the attendance of such person or persons before said arbitrator or arbitrators, or punish said person or persons for contempt in the same manner provided on February 12, 1925, for securing the attendance of witnesses or their punishment for neglect or refusal to attend in the courts of the United States.

§ 8. Proceedings Begun by Libel in Admiralty and Seizure of Vessel or Property

If the basis of jurisdiction be a cause of action otherwise justiciable in admiralty, then, notwithstanding anything herein to the contrary the party claiming to be aggrieved may begin his proceeding hereunder by libel and seizure of the vessel or other property of the other party according to the usual course of admiralty proceedings, and the court shall then have jurisdiction to direct the parties to proceed with the arbitration and shall retain jurisdiction to enter its decree upon the award.

§ 9. **Award of Arbitrators; Confirmation; Jurisdiction; Procedure**

If the parties in their agreement have agreed that a judgment of the court shall be entered upon the award made pursuant to the arbitration, and shall specify the court, then at any time within one year after the award is made any party to the arbitration may apply to the court so specified for an order confirming the award, and thereupon the court must grant such an order unless the award is vacated, modified, or corrected as prescribed in sections 10 and 11 of this title. If no court is specified in the agreement of the parties, then such application may be made to the United States court in and for the district within which such award was made. Notice of the application shall be served upon the adverse party, and thereupon the court shall have jurisdiction of such party as though he had appeared generally in the proceeding. If the adverse party is a resident of the district within which the award was made, such service shall be made upon the adverse party or his attorney as prescribed by law for service of notice of motion in an action in the same court. If the adverse party shall be a nonresident, then the notice of the application shall be served by the marshal of any district within which the adverse party may be found in like manner as other process of the court.

§ 10. Same; Vacation; Grounds; Rehearing

In either of the following cases the United States court in and for the district wherein the award was made may make an order vacating the award upon the application of any party to the arbitration—

(a) Where the award was procured by corruption, fraud, or undue means.

(b) Where there was evident partiality or corruption in the arbitrators, or either of them.

(c) Where the arbitrators were guilty of misconduct in refusing to postpone the hearing, upon sufficient cause shown, or in refusing to hear evidence pertinent and material to the controversy; or of any other misbehavior by which the rights of any party have been prejudiced.

(d) Where the arbitrators exceeded their powers, or so imperfectly executed them that a mutual, final, and definite award upon the subject matter submitted was not made.

(e) Where an award is vacated and the time within which the agreement required the award to be made has not expired the court may, in its discretion, direct a rehearing by the arbitrators.

§ 11. Same;   Modification   or   Correction; Grounds; Order

In either of the following cases the United States court in and for the district wherein the award was made may make an order modifying or correcting the award upon the application of any party to the arbitration—

(a) Where there was an evident material miscalculation of figures or an evident material mistake in the description of any person, thing, or property referred to in the award.

(b) Where the arbitrators have awarded upon a matter not submitted to them, unless it is a matter not affecting the merits of the decision upon the matter submitted.

(c) Where the award is imperfect in matter of form not affecting the merits of the controversy.

The order may modify and correct the award, so as to effect the intent thereof and promote justice between the parties.

§ 12. Notice of Motions to Vacate or Modify; Service; Stay of Proceedings

Notice of a motion to vacate, modify, or correct an award must be served upon the adverse party or his attorney within three months after the award is filed or delivered. If the adverse party is a resident of the district within which the award was made, such service shall be made upon the adverse party or his attorney as prescribed by law for service of notice of motion in an action in the same court. If the adverse party shall be a nonresident then the notice of the application shall be served by the marshal of any district within which the adverse party may be found in like manner as other process of the court. For the purposes of the motion any judge who might make an order to stay the proceedings in an action brought in the same court may make an order, to be served with the notice of motion, staying the proceedings of the adverse party to enforce the award.

§ 13. **Papers Filed with Order on Motions; Judgment; Docketing; Force and Effect; Enforcement**

The party moving for an order confirming, modifying, or correcting an award shall, at the time such order is filed with the clerk for the entry of judgment thereon, also file the following papers with the clerk:

(a) The agreement; the selection or appointment, if any, of an additional arbitrator or umpire; and each written extension of the time, if any, within which to make the award.

(b) The award.

(c) Each notice, affidavit, or other paper used upon an application to confirm, modify, or correct the award, and a copy of each order of the court upon such an application.

The judgment shall be docketed as if it was rendered in an action.

The judgment so entered shall have the same force and effect, in all respects, as, and be subject to all the provisions of law relating to, a judgment in an action; and it may be enforced as if it had been rendered in an action in the court in which it is entered.

§ 14.   Contracts Not Affected

This title shall not apply to contracts made prior to January 1, 1926.

APPENDIX 7

PROPOSED UNIFORM ARBITRATION ACT

(Adopted by the National Conference of the Commissioners on Uniform State Laws in 1955 and amended in 1956, and approved by the House of Delegates of the American Bar Association on August 26, 1955 and August 30, 1956.)

ACT RELATING TO ARBITRATION AND TO MAKE UNIFORM THE LAW WITH REFERENCE THERETO

SECTION 1. (*Validity of Arbitration Agreement.*)

A written agreement to submit any existing controversy to arbitration or a provision in a written contract to submit to arbitration any controversy thereafter arising between the parties is valid, enforceable and irrevocable, save upon such grounds as exist at law or in equity for the revocation of any contract. This act also applies to arbitration agreements between employers and employees or between their respective representatives (unless otherwise provided in the agreement.)

SECTION 2. (*Proceedings to Compel or Stay Arbitration.*)

(a) On application of a party showing an agreement described in Section 1, and the opposing party's refusal to arbitrate, the Court shall order the parties to proceed with arbitration, but if the opposing party denies the existence of the agreement to arbitrate, the Court shall proceed summarily to the determination of the issue so raised and shall order arbitration if found for the moving party, otherwise, the application shall be denied.

(b) On application, the court may stay an arbitration proceeding commenced or threatened on a showing that there is no agreement to arbitrate. Such an issue, when in substantial and bona fide dispute, shall be forthwith and summarily tried and the stay ordered if found for the moving party. If found for the opposing party, the court shall order the parties to proceed to arbitration.

(c) If an issue referable to arbitration under the alleged agreement is involved in action or proceeding pending in a court having jurisdiction to hear applications under subdivision (a) of this Section, the application shall be made therein. Otherwise and subject to Section 18, the application may be made in any court of competent jurisdiction.

(d) Any action or proceeding involving an issue subject to arbitration shall be stayed if an order for arbitration or an application therefor has been made under this section or, if the issue is severable, the stay may be with respect thereto only. When the application is made in such action or proceeding, the order for arbitration shall include such stay.

(e) An order for arbitration shall not be refused on the ground that the claim in issue lacks merit or bona fides or because any fault or grounds for the claim sought to be arbitrated have not been shown.

SECTION 3. (*Appointment of Arbitrators by Court.*) If the arbitration agreement provides a method of appointment of arbitrators, this method shall be followed. In the absence thereof, or if the agreed method fails or for any reason cannot be followed, or when an arbitrator appointed fails or is unable to act and his successor has not been duly appointed, the court on application of a party shall appoint one or more arbitrators. An arbitrator so appointed has all the powers of one specifically named in the agreement.

SECTION 4. (*Majority Action by Arbitrators.*) The powers of the arbitrators may be exercised by a majority unless otherwise provided by the agreement or by this act.

SECTION 5. (*Hearing.*) Unless otherwise provided by the agreement:

(a) The arbitrators shall appoint a time and place for the hearing and cause notification to the parties to be served personally or by registered mail not less than five days before the hearing. Appearance at the hearing waives such notice. The arbitrators may adjourn the hearing from time to time as necessary and, on request of a party and for good cause, or upon their own motion may postpone the hearing to a time not later than the date fixed by the agreement for making the award unless the parties consent to a later date. The arbitrators may hear and determine the controversy upon the evidence produced notwithstanding the failure of a party duly notified to appear. The court on application may direct the arbitrators to proceed promptly with the hearing and determination of the controversy.

(b) The parties are entitled to be heard, to present evidence material to the controversy and to cross-examine witnesses appearing at the hearing.

(c) The hearing shall be conducted by all the arbitrators but a majority may determine any question and render a final award. If, during the course of the hearing, an arbitrator for any reason ceases to act, the remaining arbitrator or arbitrators appointed to act as neutrals may continue with the hearing and determination of the controversy.

SECTION 6.   (*Representation by Attorney.*)   A party has the right to be represented by an attorney at any proceeding or hearing under this act.   A waiver thereof prior to the proceeding or hearing is ineffective.

SECTION 7.   (*Witnesses, Subpoenas, Depositions.*)

(a) The arbitrators may issue (cause to be issued) subpoenas for the attendance of witnesses and for the production of books, records, documents and other evidence, and shall have the power to administer oaths.   Subpoenas so issued shall be served, and upon application to the Court by a party or the arbitrators, enforced, in the manner provided by law for the service and enforcement of subpoenas in a civil action.

(b) On application of a party and for use as evidence, the arbitrators may permit a deposition to be taken, in the manner and upon the terms designated by the arbitrators, of a witness who cannot be subpoenaed or is unable to attend the hearing.

(c)   All provisions of law compelling a person under subpoena to testify are applicable.

(d) Fees for attendance as a witness shall be the same as for a witness in the _____ Court.

SECTION 8.   (*Award.*)

(a) The award shall be in writing and signed by the arbitrators joining in the award. The arbitrators shall deliver a copy to each party personally or by registered mail, or as provided in the agreement.

(b) An award shall be made within the time fixed therefor by the agreement or, if not so fixed, within such time as the court orders on application of a party. The parties may extend the time in writing either before or after the expiration thereof. A party waives the objection that an award was not made within the time required unless he notifies the arbitrators of his objection prior to the delivery of the award to him.

SECTION 9.   (*Change of Award by Arbitrators.*) On application of a party or, if an application to the court is pending under Sections 11, 12 or 13, on submission to the arbitrators by the court under such conditions as the court may order, the arbitrators may modify or correct the award upon the grounds stated in paragraphs (1) and (3) of subdivision (a) of Section 13, or for the purpose of clarifying the award. The application shall be made within twenty days after delivery of the award to the applicant. Written notice thereof shall be given forthwith to the opposing party, stating he must serve his objections thereto, if any, within ten days from the notice. The award so modified or corrected is subject to the provisions of Sections 11, 12 and 13.

SECTION 10. (*Fees and Expenses of Arbitration.*) Unless otherwise provided in the agreement to arbitrate, the arbitrators' expenses and fees, together with other expenses, not including counsel fees, incurred in the conduct of the arbitration, shall be paid as provided in the award.

SECTION 11. (*Confirmation of an Award.*) Upon application of a party, the court shall confirm an award, unless within the time limits hereinafter imposed grounds are urged for vacating or modifying or correcting the award, in which case the court shall proceed as provided in Sections 12 and 13.

SECTION 12. (*Vacating an Award.*)

(a) Upon application of a party, the court shall vacate an award where:

> (1) The award was procured by corruption, fraud or other undue means;

> (2) There was evident partiality by an arbitrator appointed as a neutral or corruption in any of the arbitrators or misconduct prejudicing the rights of any party;

> (3) The arbitrators exceeded their powers;

> (4) The arbitrators refused to postpone the hearing upon sufficient cause being

shown therefor or refused to hear evidence material to the controversy or otherwise so conducted the hearing, contrary to the provisions of Section 5, as to prejudice substantially the rights of a party; or

(5) There was no arbitration agreement and the issue was not adversely determined in proceedings under Section 2 and the party did not participate in the arbitration hearing without raising the objection;

But the fact that the relief was such that it could not or would not be granted by a court of law or equity is not ground for vacating or refusing to confirm the award.

(b) An application under this Section shall be made within ninety days after delivery of a copy of the award to the applicant, except that, if predicated upon corruption, fraud or other undue means, it shall be made within ninety days after such grounds are known or should have been known.

(c) In vacating the award on grounds other than stated in clause (5) of Subsection (a) the court may order a rehearing before new arbitrators chosen as provided in the agreement, or in the absence thereof, by the court in accordance with Section 3, or, if the award is vacated on grounds set forth in clauses (3), and (4) of Subsection (a) the court may order a rehearing before the arbitrators who made the award or their successors appointed in accordance with Section 3. The time within which the agreement requires the award to be made is applicable to the rehearing and commences from the date of the order.

(d) If the application to vacate is denied and no motion to modify or correct the award is pending, the court shall confirm the award.

SECTION 13. (*Modification or Correction of Award.*)

(a) Upon application made within ninety days after delivery of a copy of the award to the applicant, the court shall modify or correct the award where:

(1) There was an evident miscalculation of figures or an evident mistake in the description of any person, thing or property referred to in the award;

(2) The arbitrators have awarded upon a matter not submitted to them and the award may be corrected without affecting the merits of the decision upon the issues submitted; or

(3) The award is imperfect in a matter of form, not affecting the merits of the controversy.

(b) If the application is granted, the court shall modify and correct the award so as to effect its intent and shall confirm the award as so modified and corrected. Otherwise, the court shall confirm the award as made.

(c) An application to modify or correct an award may be joined in the alternative with an application to vacate the award.

SECTION 14. (*Judgment or Decree on Award.*) Upon the granting of an order confirming, modifying or correcting an award, judgment or decree shall be entered in conformity therewith and be enforced as any other judgment or decree. Costs of the application and of the proceedings subsequent thereto, and disbursements may be awarded by the court.

* [SECTION 15. (*Judgment Roll, Docketing.*)

(a) On entry of judgment or decree, the clerk shall prepare the judgment roll consisting, to the extent filed, of the following:

(1) The agreement and each written extension of the time within which to make the award;

(2) The award;

(3) A copy of the order confirming, modifying or correcting the award; and

---

* *Brackets and parenthesis enclose language which the Commissioners suggest may be used by those States desiring to do so.*

(4) A copy of the judgment or decree.

(b) The judgment or decree may be docketed as if rendered in an action.]

SECTION 16. (*Applications to Court.*) Except as otherwise provided, an application to the court under this act shall be by motion and shall be heard in the manner and upon the notice provided by law or rule of court for the making and hearing of motions. Unless the parties have agreed otherwise, notice of an initial application for an order shall be served in the manner provided by law for the service of a summons in an action.

SECTION 17. (*Court, Jurisdiction.*) The term "court" means any court of competent jurisdiction of this State. The making of an agreement described in Section 1 providing for arbitration in this State confers jurisdiction on the court to enforce the agreement under this Act and to enter judgment on an award thereunder.

SECTION 18. (*Venue.*) An initial application shall be made to the court of the (county) in which the agreement provides the arbitration hearing shall be held or, if the hearing has been held, in the county in which it was held. Otherwise the application shall be made in the (county) where the adverse party resides or has a place of business or, if he has no residence or place of business in this State, to the court of any (county). All subsequent applications shall be made to the court hearing the initial application unless the court otherwise directs.

SECTION 19. (*Appeals.*)

(a) An appeal may be taken from:

(1) An order denying an application to compel arbitration made under Section 2;

(2) An order granting an application to stay arbitration made under Section 2(b);

(3) An order confirming or denying confirmation of an award;

(4) An order modifying or correcting an award;

(5) An order vacating an award without directing a rehearing; or

(6) A judgment or decree entered pursuant to the provisions of this act.

(b) The appeal shall be taken in the manner and to the same extent as from orders or judgments in a civil action.

SECTION 20. (*Act Not Retroactive.*) This act applies only to agreements made subsequent to the taking effect of this act.

SECTION 21. (*Uniformity of Interpretation.*) This act shall be so construed as to effectuate its general purpose to make uniform the law of those states which enact it.

SECTION 22. (*Constitutionality.*) If any provision of this act or the application thereof to any person or circumstance is held invalid, the invalidity shall not affect other provisions or applications of the act which can be given without the invalid provision or application, and to this end the provisions of this act are severable.

SECTION 23. (*Short Title.*) This act may be cited as the Uniform Arbitration Act.

SECTION 24. (*Repeal.*) All acts or parts of acts which are inconsistent with the provisions of this act are hereby repealed.

SECTION 25. (*Time of Taking Effect.*) This act shall take effect _____.

INDEX

References are to Pages

INDEX

INDEX

INDEX

[*353*]

INDEX